Reprogram Your Mind

Neuroscience Reveals How Psilocybin Increases Emotional Healing

Sarah R. Grace

sarahrgrace.com

BOUNDLESS PUBLISHING

Is Psilocybin Assisted Psychotherapy Right for You?

Have you experienced:

- a life-threatening event
- death of a loved one
- military combat
- severe childhood trauma
- a terminal diagnosis
- treatment-resistant depression
- addiction

Is this trauma still negatively impacting your life?

Have you tried multiple psychotherapists, psychiatrists, antidepressants, or antianxiety medications? And you're still stuck, depressed or anxious?

Then go to my website, **sarahrgrace.com**, for a list of the top 5 reasons why psilocybin assisted psychotherapy could help you.

This book is dedicated to Donna, a dear friend who will be missed.

Sadly, she didn't have access to these, or similar resources, and her life was unnecessarily cut short.

Love goes far beyond what you call the grave.

~ Edgar Cayce

Table of Contents

Introduction

"Hope is the thing with feathers that perches in the soul,

And sings the tune without the words, and never stops at all."

—Emily Dickinson

Imagine spending 15 years covering crime as part of your job. Imagine seeing blood everywhere, hearing the screams of mothers who have lost their sons, and getting used to it. Imagine not getting used to it but pretending that you are. Imagine seeing the most heinous crimes being committed and acting like you can take it. For 15 years.

This was the story of Kevin Deutsch, who had worked as a crime journalist for various reported newspapers before the job started taking its toll on him. To be fair, it began much sooner, but being able to digest these unimaginable events is a hallmark of a successful crime journalist. The cracks were finally beginning to show. Deutsch struggled with insomnia as well as nightmares. The people that had died in front of him or people he had known who had died violent deaths, they all came to visit him in these nightmares.

Little by little, he stopped going out for anything other than work and felt paranoid about his life as well as his family's. It was clear that he was suffering from post-traumatic stress disorder (PTSD). The biggest challenge for him was to deal with PTSD while still working at his job. Add to that the damage to his reputation owing to a social media scandal, in true social media fashion. He was scrambling for life and peace. After having tried various therapies, none of which worked, he finally tried psilocybin. As someone who had covered the drug war for years, he was initially skeptical about trying out a psychedelic as part of psychotherapy, but after doing his research, he felt hopeful for the first time in a long time.

After he tried psilocybin for the first time, he experienced healing like never before. He was able to meet his demons, the people who had died, and they were able to meet him in an atmosphere of love and forgiveness. The visions that he saw also made it possible for him to reconcile with his fear of death. Once he realized that death was not the end, he felt more at peace with the possibility of facing it someday.

While he still struggles with PTSD symptoms now and then, he has experienced immense healing since he first took psilocybin.

Deutsch's story is a story of hope, and it can be yours too.

We contain many hidden parts within ourselves but are apprehensive of exploring them. We're worried about what we might stumble upon, never mind if it is good or bad. The unknown scares us, especially if that unknown is within us. At the same time, this world, this wild and wonderful world of ours, is full of people who have known and experienced things that seem impossible. We've known scientists, artists, and mystics who have shattered stereotypes, broken barriers, and ushered in new and previously unimagined realities for the rest of us.

Have they faced ridicule when they started? More often than not, yes. Have they faced resistance from the establishment? Of course. Have they sometimes felt lonely on their paths? It would seem so. Have they given up? Almost, but not quite. We owe these intrepid explorers so much of what we see in our lives today and maybe even take for granted. Now that we are experiencing the benefits of their discoveries or living in a world shaped by their once revolutionary, and even incendiary, ideas, we might be forgiven if we fail to understand the journeys taken by some for the rest of us.

These journeys have been marked by a lot of work, faith, and hope. The journey that we're about to undertake is also marked by hope. But don't get me wrong. This isn't blind hope that I'm talking about but hope that is built on concrete facts and real stories. If hope seems like the purview of the mystic or the priest, it isn't. In fact, as we shall soon see, it is the material world and the people that inhabit it which have made this book a possibility.

The Magic in the Mushrooms

I've mentioned before that you don't have to be spiritually inclined to appreciate this book. That is because I am not asking you to have blind faith. Instead, I am asking you to read with an open mind about fungi that have existed for millennia and decide for yourself if magic is real. Who is this book for? It is for those willing to have their perspectives challenged about psychedelics and their abilities. It is for those who know nothing about this world and are both curious and scared about entering it. But most of all, it is for people who have given up hope. Why do I say that? Let me explain.

The world is beset with difficulties like never before. The Covid-19 pandemic has upended our view of the world as well as of ourselves. Not to sound too much like someone hell-bent on finding the silver lining in every cloud, but this is a time when our collective consciousness is registering another pandemic of an equal, if not larger, scale. This pandemic has been raging on for decades but has somehow never been on the radar of the world as much as now. It has affected millions and caused widespread suffering, yet the ones afflicted have mostly felt lonely and misunderstood. The pandemic I'm referring to is the mental health pandemic.

For many years, people have suffered in silence from various illnesses of the mind, including anxiety, depression, PTSD, obsessive compulsive disorder (OCD), and addictions. The World Health Organization states that more than 700,000 people commit suicide every year. In recent years, there has been growing awareness of these diseases, and the mental health community has also worked to find solutions. That being said, the situation is far from optimal. Many people struggle for years with debilitating symptoms without any hope in sight. Many have visited multiple doctors, sought support in various places, and tried a whole range of medications without seeing improvements and, in some cases, dealing with the side-effects of the pharmacological drugs. Even when they have felt some temporary relief, it has been overshadowed by the knowledge that the effects won't last long. It has been a continuous, tiring, and hopeless journey for many.

If you, dear reader, are one of those people, then your cynicism is understandable. After all, it is said that deep down every cynic is a disappointed idealist or a hopeless romantic. Even if you don't think so, you know what it means to be given hope, only to have it quashed repeatedly. I wouldn't wish this vicious cycle on anyone, but I know all too well how it feels.

This book does not claim to be the answer to all your problems, but it does hope to shine a light in the dark, never-ending tunnel you find yourself in. Specifically, I want to introduce you to the psychoactive substance called psilocybin which is present in these mushrooms and to its immense potential for emotional and mental healing and well-being. I understand this sounds like a tall claim. I'm also aware of the common perceptions regarding psychedelics, in general, held by both the public as a whole, as well as some members of the scientific community. I am not here to dispute science using faith or spirituality. In fact, I firmly believe that one cannot exist without the other. Why, then, am I confident about espousing the benefits of psilocybin? Mostly because we now have the science to prove it.

Through this book, I plan to chart the trajectory of this magical and medicinal compound. The story of how it was discovered, how it gained prominence, how it became a threat, and how it saw a resurgence among the very communities that once wanted nothing to do with it is as fascinating as the compound itself. The psychedelic community has never had a dearth of anecdotal evidence. Many people have undertaken this journey and come out more than eager to share their experiences with it. Those stories are valuable and will form a large part of this book as well. That being said, I also understand why clinical evidence is essential for people to believe in its benefits.

Fortunately, the last couple of decades have been revolutionary in the field of psychedelic research. More specifically, there have been various credible and reputable studies and trials examining the positive effects of psychedelics in general and psilocybin, in particular, on a wide range of participants. Some have been focused on mystical experiences and the concept of transcendence, which I'll also investigate in the later chapters. Many have focused on psychotherapy, or the use of psilocybin to improve the mental and emotional well-being of people who have struggled with various mental health disorders for years. I will delve deep into that fascinating research as well.

The last part of the book is dedicated to understanding the legality of using this drug, the various laws and rules that govern its research as well as usage, and the underground movement that has been influenced by these laws. I will also shed some light on the numerous possibilities for psilocybin at present and in the future, both for clinical research and therapeutic purposes. These possibilities are shaping the realms of law and business in many parts of the US as well as the world. In fact, the entire book is a launching pad of possibilities, for you and many others in the world.

Before I begin, I want to make it clear that this book is not a license to use psilocybin indiscriminately or to infringe upon the laws of any country. It is a report on the nature and workings of psilocybin as medicine. I want you to read the book and come out of it with hope for the future. I hope that you see possibilities where once you were pessimistic, reach out to people working actively in this field and have discussions about what these findings mean for you, and even volunteer to participate in legitimate trials and see for yourself the benefits we talk about here. Psilocybin has been known to evoke a feeling of openness in people who consume it. I hope that learning about its many benefits will make you more open and receptive to it as well. Let the healing begin!

Chapter 1:

Psilocybin: History, Mystery, and Chemistry

Before we delve deep into the history and uses of psilocybin let us understand what psychedelics are and why they hold such promise for our future.

Psychedelics are a class of psychoactive substances also known as hallucinogens. They produce changes in mood, perception, and cognitive processes. With a high enough dose, they can trigger non-ordinary states of consciousness through serotonin 2A receptors. Psychedelics are known to affect all our senses, and their exact mode of working is still being studied by various researchers all over the world.

Many people know of psychedelics because of their association with the counterculture and their depiction in popular media of the 1960s and '70s. There is an incomplete and often misleading image of psychedelics in the minds of most of us which keeps us from realizing the full potential of these truly magical compounds. Thankfully, there has been a renewed interest in these compounds in the past couple of decades. The scientific and academic community has started investigating the effects of these compounds in different areas and is seeing promising results that can re-envision the future of healing, psychiatry, and psychotherapy. In the later chapters, we shall learn more about the exciting research being conducted on psilocybin.

There are many different kinds of psychedelics. Some occur naturally in trees, vines, fungi, and leaves, while others are synthesized in laboratories. Some of the most well-known ones are:

- Lysergic acid diethylamide (LSD)—It is made from a substance found in ergot, which is a fungus that infects rye.
- Peyote—Also known as *Lophophora williamsii*, it is a very small and slow-growing cactus which is also a potent psychedelic. It grows as buttons close to the ground instead of the usual columns.
- Mescaline—It is derived from the Mexican peyote and San Pedro cacti.
- Entactogens—This is a term used by psychiatrists to classify 3,4-methylenedioxymethamphetamine (MDMA) and related psychedelics.
- Psilocybin—This is a naturally occurring substance found in various species of mushrooms all over the world.
- Dimethyltryptamine (DMT)—Structurally similar to psilocin, an alkaloid found in psilocybin mushrooms, it is a naturally occurring component of many plants but can also be synthesized in the laboratory.

Apart from these, many other compounds are being discovered as psychedelics.

A Rose by Any Other Name?

Before we begin to learn about the specific history of psilocybin, let us discuss the effect that nomenclature has on perceptions, especially in the case of psychedelics. Why is that important? Because the history as well as the fate of psychedelics is inextricably tied to perceptions. Of course, they are known to alter perceptions of those who consume them, but in a twist of fate, we have a profound effect on how they are perceived as well. What do I mean by that? We only need to look at the different names given to this class of compounds to understand that.

Many people in the scientific and academic community still prefer the term **hallucinogens** to describe this class of compounds. A hallucinogen is a psychoactive compound that causes hallucinations, perceptual anomalies, and substantial changes in thoughts, emotions, and consciousness. It is used to classify drugs that produce what is commonly known as a "trip" or "journey."

In the earlier days of psychedelic research, when little was understood about these compounds, they were known as **psychotomimetics**. This term implies that psychedelics produce not just hallucinations, but also mimic the symptoms of psychosis such as delusions and/or delirium. This is a narrow understanding that is tinged with fear and paranoia. When you call them psychotomimetics, these compounds can do no good.

In fact, many of the psychonauts (ancient Greek term meaning sailor of the soul, spirit or mind) that we'll learn about in a later chapter found the term pejorative and harmful to the image they wanted policy makers as well as the general public to have regarding these compounds.

In direct contrast to this is the term **entheogen**. This is a neologism coined by a group of ethnobotanists and scholars of mythology in 1979 to counter the deterioration in the perception of these compounds during the "hippie" subculture of the 1960s and '70s. They wanted to give credit to the role of psychedelics in early cultures and religions. The term translates to "God within us." In this context, psychoactive plants that are ingested provide us a divine experience like no other. As you can see, the term invokes reverence and awe rather than frivolousness. Many of the researchers still feel that this term is best limited to experiences that are purely spiritual in nature so as not to tarnish it by association.

When psychiatrist Humphry Osmond was looking for a term other than hallucinogens to allude to the psychotherapeutic uses of these substances in 1956, he asked the famous British author Aldous Huxley for help. Huxley, who was a supporter of the therapeutic uses of these substances, suggested the term **phanerothyme**. This word was derived from the Greek words for "manifest" and "spirit." Osmond then coined the term **psychedelic**, as it was clear, sounded better, and free from any associations. Psychedelic means "mind-manifesting."

When we think of these compounds as mind-manifesting, we do more than just name them. We bestow them with a potential that is crucial to fields like psychiatry and psychotherapy. It is a neutral term but not a weak one. As we shall see in the later chapters, psychedelics are manifesting realities that were previously unthought of.

The History and Mystery of Psilocybin

As mentioned earlier, psilocybin is a naturally occurring psychedelic produced by more than 200 species of fungi around the world. The history of these mushrooms is as mind-boggling as the effects they are said to produce. In fact, the earliest known species are over a billion years old. In 2019, paleobiologist Corentin Loron discovered a fossil species called *Ourasphaira giraldae* which many scientists believe can hold clues to how life started on land.

In fact, a theory proposed by ethnobotanist and mystic Terrence McKenna in his 1992 book *Food of the Gods* proposes the idea that these mushrooms played a direct role in human evolution. While it was earlier dismissed as a wildly improbable theory by scientists, it has recently found traction again after a talk given by mycologist Paul Stamets at the Psychedelic Science conference in April 2017.

Stoned Ape Theory

This theory posited that the evolution of our species from *Homo erectus* to *Homo sapiens* occurred due to magic mushrooms and psilocybin. More specifically, McKenna thought that we "ate our way to higher consciousness."

According to him, it was psilocybin that brought us out of our primitive world and made articulated speech and imagination possible. It was because of psilocybin that our primitive information-processing brains reorganized and made cognition possible. Cognition, in turn, was responsible for helping us create the early art, technology, and language that became markers of our civilization. According to Stamets, the major reason this theory holds ground is that some anthropologists believe that, between two million and 700,000 years ago, the *Homo erectus* brain doubled. Though the details are still up for debate, the fact remains that this theory is neither easy to prove nor disprove.

Another major issue that arises with validating this theory is the concept of consciousness itself, which is a complex topic that needs its own book. While some researchers don't want to attribute something as vast and unexplored as consciousness to a single factor, in this case, mushrooms, there is nothing to say that they might not have been an important part of the journey itself. In either case, it is a fascinating theory that highlights the influence that these fungi have on our consciousness, literally and otherwise.

In fact, we are currently at a stage where we can use our growing understanding of psilocybin and combine it with our limited understanding of consciousness to explore the implications of this theory. We have more advanced tools than before, and there are many researchers dedicated to understanding how consciousness is connected to language and cognition as well as psychedelics.

Psilocybin in Ancient Societies

There are some accounts that talk of mushrooms being depicted on cave paintings that are almost 9,000 years old. These accounts are largely unverified, but there is no doubt that psilocybin occupied a leading role in many ancient societies and cultures. In fact, as we shall soon see, the modern world owes a huge debt to one of these societies for the discovery and understanding of psilocybin.

Psilocybin in Central America—For many societies in Central America, psilocybe mushrooms were considered highly significant, so much so, that they were deemed a channel to communicate with the gods. There is a lot of indigenous artwork that even today highlights the fascination that these cultures had with these mushrooms. Remember we talked about how language shapes perceptions? Nowhere is this more apparent than in the nomenclature used by the Mayan and Aztec people. In their native language, known as *Nahuatl*, psilocybin was known as *Teonanácatl*, which translates to "flesh of the gods."

According to their religious myths, these mushrooms were given to them by their serpent god *Quetzalcoatl*, who was the creator of all life. They held various elaborate rituals which included the ingestion of psilocybin to connect with the divine as well as to heal themselves and others. Not only that, they kept elaborate records of these rituals and ceremonies through art and storytelling.

Another aspect of these ceremonies that deserves mention is the obvious parallel between them and the Christian rite of Communion or Eucharist, in which consecrated bread and wine are seen as the body and blood of Christ. When you compare that to what was called "flesh of the gods," you can see where the reverence came from. To directly commune with God is no small matter. Even more compelling is the fact that, while most established religions usually have a few original apostles who are witness to miracles or God's message and the rest of us need to have faith in them, these ceremonies allowed everyone who participated to be able to directly communicate with God. If there was a miracle, everyone was a part of it. If God wanted to tell you something, all you had to do was ingest "the flesh of the gods." In these ceremonies, the concept of faith itself was challenged because you didn't need to have faith in what you could see and experience firsthand.

This is also why these ceremonies and the documents related to them were destroyed by Spanish missionaries in the 1500s – but more on that shortly.

Psychoactive mushrooms in Siberia—Eurasian Shamen are known to have used psychoactive mushrooms for religious purposes. This practice is especially well-documented in Siberia, where many groups including the Khanty (Ostyaks), Selkup (Southern Samoyeds), Nganasan (Taimyr Samoyeds), and Ket (Yenisey Ostyaks) took part in an interesting tradition. Thousands of years old, this tradition includes sipping on the hallucinogenic urine of reindeer who eat the red and white spotted *Amanita muscaria* mushroom, also known as *fly agaric* or *fly amanita*. The effects of these mushrooms differ from those that contain psilocybin, but they are also deeply rooted in spirituality. It is said that these mushrooms conjure up the *Fly Agaric* spirits, also known as *wapaq*. These spirits are said to bear the shape of mushrooms and are mischievous in nature, playing pranks on those that consume the mushrooms.

Food of the Gods in Egypt—Along with other civilizations, Egypt also has a deep connection with psychoactive mushrooms. Their artwork depicts the significance of mushrooms in their lives. In fact, they believed that, since mushrooms didn't sprout from seeds, they were a gift from Osiris, their god of fertility, agriculture, and the afterlife. Since he is believed to have embedded the mushrooms in the ground, they were known as "food of the gods" or "grain of the gods." Consequently, only the priesthood and upper classes were given access to these godly mushrooms.

Eleusinian Psychedelic Rebirth Rites in Greece—There is well-documented use of psychedelic mushrooms in ancient Greece through psychedelic rituals called the "Eleusinian Mysteries." These rituals were not only widely accepted but were celebrated in the ancient societies. In fact, everyone—men, women, slaves, scholars, emperors—were welcome to drink *kykeon*. This magic potion and the ritual connected to it was supposed to connect people with Demeter, the goddess of grain. Therefore, these ceremonies were usually held to celebrate harvest cycles and the resulting communion with the divine.

These ceremonies were conducted in secret but were attended by many people and were supposed to be incredibly healing and transformative experiences for those that participated in them. The drink was supposed to get its potency from ergot fungus and psychedelic mushrooms and was known as the "antidote to isolation." This designation could be because drinking *kykeon* made them feel connected to something beyond themselves (a description that many psychedelic users will agree with) or because this ceremony itself gave them a unique opportunity to connect with their friends and family, with all of them bathing in its afterglow. The afterglow itself is a state that many people swear by. It is commonly referred to as the positive physical and mental effects that linger after the main effects, or the peak experience, of the psychedelic have subsided. While some people describe it as a feeling of detachment from the past as well as guilt and anxiety, others report an elevation in mood and clarity. As can be seen, the effect is highly desirable and can lead to one experiencing a rare feeling of harmony with themselves and others. It makes sense, then, that these ceremonies brought everyone together. There was only one caveat: In order to participate, you needed to speak fluent Greek and must never have committed a murder. It was as simple as that.

The Quest for Immortality in Vedic culture—The *Rig Veda* is an ancient text belonging to the Vedic religion which contains over 100 mentions of the Soma plant. The ancient Indo-Aryans considered this plant as an elixir of strength and health. At the same time, it was supposed to bring the people who consumed the drink in direct communion with the gods. Some scholars propose that the ancient Soma cult was created around the pursuit of immortality by the people who ingested the soma plant. This cult eventually died out, and the actual identity of the soma plant has never been revealed. There has been a lot of debate over what the original plant was and why its identity has been steeped in mystery for over 3000 years. Some historians suggest that the abandonment of the original plant and the use of surrogates was because its ingestion became forbidden. According to ethnomycologist R. Gordon Wasson, the original plant was the hallucinogenic *Amanita muscaria* mushroom.

Mushrooms in Indo-European cultures—The use of Soma (or the *Amanita muscaria* mushroom) wasn't confined to the Vedic culture. In *Avesta*, the Persian religious text, Soma is referred to as "Haoma.") According to Persian *Magis*, or fire worshippers, Hoama was a ritual elixir for the deity known as *Ahur Mazda*. Similar mushroom-centered rituals were spread to other Indo-European tribes and cultures of the west, which dominated the Asian steppes in ancient times. The Norse, Celtic, and Druid rituals also contained the use of these psychedelic drinks.

It is believed that Druids prepared fly-agaric for consumption, and that the hallucinations induced by it were a way for them to obtain knowledge and enlightenment. Even today, sweat houses are found all over Ireland, which is where Druids were believed to have sat after consuming these mushrooms. The author Peter Lambron Wilson wrote *Ploughing the Clouds*, a book which describes Indo-Europeans using psychedelic drugs in their worship rituals. He also suggested that the mystical experiences that were a part of these rituals were the origin of pagan religions in Ireland.

The Stories Told in Stones—As we can see, no ancient civilization was untouched by the effect of these mushrooms. In fact, there are several stone sculptures in El Salvador, Guatemala, and Mexico known as mushroom idols or mushroom stones. In 1952, archaeologists at the Maya site of Kaminaljuyu on the outskirts of Guatemala City found a tripod stone depicting a mushroom with a jaguar effigy at its base. Studies are underway to determine if the mushrooms depicted on these sculptures were indeed the *Amanita muscaria* mushrooms. Wasson believed that it was through these sculptures that the Maya and Aztec people told stories of their rituals.

Introduction of Psilocybin to the New World

As we can see, much of the West had remained largely unaware of the existence of these rituals as well as the mushrooms that made them possible. In the 1500s, Spanish missionaries in Mexico had an opportunity to witness the hallucinogenic rituals of the Aztecs. Remember the discussion we had about the parallels between these rituals and the Eucharist? The similarities didn't go unnoticed by these missionaries either. Reportedly, they were disgusted at the beliefs that these rituals espoused and found them to be a threat to Christianity. Whether it was disbelief, disgust, or fear we shall never know. What we do know is that they destroyed whatever evidence of these rituals they could find, be it art, sculpture, or written records. Not only that, they didn't attempt to keep proper records of their own experiences and banished all forms of mushroom use.

To understand the history of psychedelics is to understand the fear and trepidation that has always surrounded them. When we realize that psychedelics have been prohibited not only in the recent past but throughout history, two things become apparent. For one, we realize that this is a cycle that goes through peaks and troughs. The euphoria surrounding these substances is followed by paranoia which drives the entire movement underground. The resurgence in interest that we're witnessing in current times is also part of the cycle. Whether we will be able to break the cycle and sustain the work being done in this field remains to be seen. But we have hope. In fact, even during the Dark Ages of psychedelics, there were a few psychonauts who didn't lose hope, perhaps because they understood that this cycle has occurred in the past and they only had to wait for the atmosphere to be positive again. And that is the second thing that history teaches us: that there is always hope.

The ban on mushroom worship didn't end the rituals but only drove them underground. At the same time, there were some missionaries who understood the significance of what they were witnessing and were moved rather than repulsed. One such person who was responsible for the introduction of psilocybin to the modern world was a sixteenth-century Spanish Franciscan friar Bernardino de Sahagún. In 1529, he travelled to Mexico (then known as New Spain) to conduct ethnographic studies. In the process, he learned *Nahuatl* and spent more than 50 years immersing himself in the Aztec culture, beliefs, and rituals.

He noted all that he learned and experienced in a book called *Historia general de las cosas de la Nueva España*, which translates to *General History of the Things of New Spain.* The most famous existing manuscript is known as the *Florentine Codex*, which contains 2,400 pages and about 2,500 illustrations organized into 12 books. In this elaborate book, Sahagún repeatedly refers to the *Teonanácatl.*

This book was significant in confirming to the 20th-century ethnobotanists that these mushrooms existed and that they had psychedelic properties. Due to the ban on performing these rituals, there was a great debate as to whether these mushrooms existed or not. Many denied it until 1936, when Robert J. Weitlaner, an Austrian born metallurgical engineer turned Ethnologist and later a full Professor at National Institute of Anthropology and History (Mexico), was able to obtain certain specimens. Through a curious turn of events, Weitlaner sent a specimen of the mushroom to a journalist, Victor Reko, who, in turn, sent samples off to Dr. Carl Gustaf Santesson in Sweden and to the Farlow Herbarium at Harvard for chemical analysis. By the time they arrived at Harvard University, they were so badly decomposed that identification was impossible. But this event piqued the curiosity of many around him.

Two years later, his daughter, her fiancé and two others had the opportunity to attend a mushroom ceremony in Huautla (Mexico). When the group provided details of their visit, Harvard botanist Richard Evans Schultes obtained specimens of three species of sacred mushrooms in Huautla later that year and identified them as *Psilocybe caerulescens*, *Panaeolus campanulatus*, and *Stropharia cubensis*. This was the first step towards the discovery of psilocybin by US scientists. Unfortunately, due to World War II, further investigations were prevented. Fortunately for us, the story continues after the end of the war.

The First Psilocybin Psychonauts

This is a journey like no other, and so, it requires adventurers like no other. These adventurers, explorers, and intrepid spirits are known as psychonauts. Think of astronauts and how they explore space and challenge the boundaries of the known universe. Psychonauts play a similar role in the history of psychedelics. The term psychonauts is attributed to the German author Ernest Jünger in his 1970 essay titled "Approaches: Drugs and Inebriation" based on his own drug experiences. In this essay, he drew parallels between these psychedelic experiences and physical exploration. He talked about the dangers of encountering hidden "reefs." We will further discuss the kinds of experiences that psilocybin occasions, but psychonauts have played a very crucial role in helping us explore the limits of what we think is possible. This time, the universe to explore lies within each one of us, and the only way to get to know it better is to experience firsthand what it feels like to ingest these psychedelics.

The last part of this chapter is briefly dedicated to three such psychonauts who made it possible for psilocybin to enter the US laboratories as well as the public consciousness. These three personalities are interconnected in a fascinating story.

Seeking the Magic Mushroom

The story that had been temporarily halted during World War II picked up again in 1952. This time the story brings together a *curandera*, also known as a healer or Shaman in Spanish, a banker and his wife, and the man who had the first entirely uninfluenced experience with a psychedelic in the US. In 1952, Robert Gordon Wasson, who was a Vice President of Public Relations at JP Morgan & Co, and his wife Valentina Pavlovna Wasson, who was a medical professional, received a letter containing a journal article that quoted Richard Evans Schultes discussing the 16th century Mesoamerican rituals using psychoactive mushrooms. Both Wasson and his wife were amateur mycologists and had been intrigued by this field of study for decades. Wasson is a prominent figure in the history of psilocybin, especially with its introduction to the West, but he is also one of the first people to engage in mycolatry. Mycolatry is a term used to describe the study of mushroom worship in ancient civilizations and a discipline that gained prominence through Wasson's descriptions.

The Schultes article motivated Wasson and his wife to take several trips to remote villages in Mexico to find these mushrooms and see for themselves if these stories were real. This was no easy feat because Mexico was going through its own dark age of psychedelics in a way, and the villagers were understandably wary of foreigners. The ceremonies themselves were held in secret, and foreigners were almost never allowed. Then, something remarkable happened. On one of his trips to the town of Huautla de Jiménez in Oaxaca, Mexico, in 1955, Wasson, along with New York society photographer Allan Richardson, were able to convince a woman he referred to as Eva Mendez to allow them to be a part of a Mazatec ritual. This woman's real name was Maria Sabina, a well-respected *curandera.* She and her daughter together presided over this ritual, and it was the first time in recorded history that two white men were able to witness and participate in this ritual. All the adults in the ceremony ingested the mushrooms, and there was occasional chanting, singing, and apparent communication with the divine in the room. Wasson came away from this experience completely transformed and with a renewed belief that these mushrooms could help the Western world explore parts of itself that it knew nothing about and was scared of experiencing. Notably, at the time, Wasson didn't think that there were any therapeutic effects of the mushrooms. Instead, they were used to occasion mystical experiences and for divination. Therefore, if someone who was sick or dying took the mushrooms, they would get an answer as to whether they were going to live or die and, accordingly, would either resign themselves to their fate or seek treatment with renewed faith.

In 1957, *Life* magazine chronicled their experiences in a photo-essay titled "Seeking the Magic Mushroom." This was the first time that these mushrooms were introduced to a wide audience. That same year, Wasson took another expedition to Mexico, this time accompanied by French mycologist Roger Heim, who identified many of these mushrooms as belonging to the *Psilocybe* species. After going back to France, Heim cultivated these mushrooms and sent a 100 g sample of dried *Psilocybe mexicana* to a man named Albert Hoffman.

Albert Hoffman is the third and final piece of this puzzle. A revered figure in the history of psychedelics, he was a natural products chemist working at Sandoz Pharmaceuticals. His claim to fame? He had discovered the effects of LSD in 1943. He had discovered these effects by ingesting the psychedelic and was the first and only unbiased and unadulterated western individual to self-induce himself with this psychedelic experience. Why unadulterated? Because a major concern that has plagued those who try to understand psychedelic experiences in individuals is that the visions or hallucinations that are described in today's commonplace vernacular might as well have been influenced by what they have read or heard about elsewhere. We will discuss these concerns in a later chapter.

When these mushrooms reached Hoffman's laboratory, he first tried experimenting on animals such as mice or dogs and found no dramatic effects on their behavior. In fact, the first subtle effects of low-dose hallucinogens on mice were not reported until as late as 1967. Therefore, Hoffmann decided to ingest 2.4 g of these mushrooms himself to confirm if they were indeed psychoactive. Not only he, but several of his colleagues as well, volunteered to ingest these extracts that were subjected to paper chromatography and cut into bands. When the active ingredient was finally identified, Hoffmann isolated enough of the element, which was then crystalized and named psilocybin. He also identified a minor component which he named psilocin. While psilocybin is a relatively stable, white crystalline, and water-soluble material, psilocin is not water soluble and slowly decomposes at room temperature. The discovery of psilocybin brought about a new wave in psychedelic research after LSD, and we shall see how the research around psilocybin has evolved over the years.

Before we move on to the next chapter, I would like to end these accounts by noting the effect that the *Life* magazine essay had on the woman who made it all possible. Maria Sabina was a remarkable woman who had immense knowledge of the mushrooms, not through scientific research, but through the special wisdom that comes from having lived with many experiences all through her life. To protect her identity, Wasson changed her name to Eva Mendez in the article, but it didn't help her from being identified, especially by those in her community.

While the recognition she got gave her some form of financial stability, it also brought her a lot of criticism. The small town that was relatively unknown to and untouched by the West saw many personalities, famous and otherwise, frequenting it to experience the miraculous effects of these mushrooms firsthand. This led to many people blaming Maria for bringing ruin upon their village and profiting from it. Even Wasson lamented later in his life that, although his intentions were pure, he might have caused difficulties for Maria and the villagers because of all the publicity.

Since this book is about advancements and hope, let us not forget that progress usually comes at a price. We should not trifle with what others consider sacred without understanding the importance of it. Even as we move into a new era of psychedelic research and the future holds immense promise, let us not forget and respect the people who have made this possible.

Chapter 2:

Psilocybin and Clinical Research

This book is dedicated to healing through psychedelics. The first chapter showed us that healing has been central to the psychedelic experience throughout history. Why, then, are we only now seeing a heightened level of interest and study into the effects of psilocybin, in particular, and psychedelics in general? To understand this, we must understand how clinical research has progressed throughout the years.

The First Wave: 1950s to 1960s

After psilocybin was identified and synthesiżed, Sandoz Pharmaceuticals proposed the drug to be useful in psychotherapy. In order to encourage research on the same, it started distributing tablets containing 2 mg of psilocybin under the trade name Indocybin™ in 1960. They distributed the tablets to any researcher who requested them and committed to reporting the shared experiences. This was the case with LSD as well. At the time, both psychedelics were legal and enjoyed government support. Between 1960 to 1980, the government-funded research on LSD as well as psilocybin. In fact, during this period, there were more than one hundred published literature reports on the anecdotal use of psilocybin. Apart from that, psychedelics were tested on people suffering from alcohol and tobacco addictions, OCD, autistic spectrum disorders, depression, schizophrenia, and end-of-life anxiety due to terminal cancer. It was also tested on convicts and people who were perfectly healthy. In healthy individuals, tests were conducted to discover the effects on creativity. While the results were encouraging, there were a couple of issues with them.

First and foremost, almost none of these studies were controlled. What is a controlled experiment? Simply put, a controlled experiment keeps all variables constant, except for one. For example, if you want to evaluate for the effect of different soil types on plant growth, you will have to keep separate pots, each filled with a different soil type. At the same time, you would ensure that all of them receive the same exposure to sunlight, water, and other conditions. In this way, you will be able to analyze the effects purely based on the condition that is being varied. This is essential to remove any uncertainty about the results. A controlled experiment would be conducted with an experimental, as well as a control group. This was missing from most of these studies.

Another factor that led to confusion regarding the results was that the experiments were not conducted single-blind, let alone double-blind. What do these terms mean? In a single-blind experiment, researchers are aware of which participants receive the treatment and which receive the placebo. In other words, the participants in the study are unaware of what they are being administered. In a double-blind experiment, both the researchers as well as the participants remain unaware of this allotment. Why is this important, especially in psychedelic research? Psychedelics are all about influence, and for a while it seemed that psychedelic research might be too. Many of the experiments conducted during the early periods were marked by excessive enthusiasm of the researchers. Here was a drug that could potentially change how we thought about psychiatry and psychotherapy, and the enthusiasm made sense. But it also made the experiments less valid. You don't want either the participants or your researchers to go into these studies having biases in their mind. For these studies to be independent, a double-blind condition, along with a placebo condition, was essential. Again, this was not the case for many of the studies. In our chapter on psychotherapy, we will go into greater detail about two central aspects of the experience known as "set" and "setting." This will make it clearer why robust scientific research has remained a challenge for so long in this field.

There were two experiments conducted around psilocybin in this period that deserve special mention.

Marsh Chapel Experiment

While most of the early studies conducted during this time were devoid of rigor, the Marsh Chapel Experiment was one of the most rigorous and influential of them. Also known as the Good Friday Experiment, it was conducted in 1962 by Walter Panhke. He was a psychiatrist and minister working on a PhD dissertation under Timothy Leary at Harvard University at the time. Timothy Leary is one of the most influential figures in psychedelics, though not always in a positive light. That being said, his contributions in shining a spotlight on both LSD and psilocybin cannot be discounted.

The Marsh Chapel experiment was designed as a double-blind controlled study in which twenty divinity students were each given a capsule of white powder before the Good Friday service at Marsh Chapel in Boston University. Ten of the capsules contained psilocybin, and the other ten received an active placebo (nicotinic acid). While eight of the ten students who received psilocybin reported having a mystical experience, only one of these in the control group experienced a feeling of "sacredness" and a "sense of peace." It is worth noting that while the study was designed to be double-blind, it was not difficult to tell which students had taken psilocybin and were therefore experiencing a full-blown trip. The conclusion that Pahnke derived from the experiences of the eight students was that they were having mystical experiences no different from those experienced by mystics such as Rumi, St. Theresa of Avila, or Buddha. Two things are to be noted about this experiment. Firstly, it wasn't designed to evaluate for therapeutic effects, but, instead, for mystical experiences. Secondly, it was concluded that a mystical experience on a drug is no different from a mystical experience through any other means such as prayer or higher forms of meditation.

A follow-up to the experiment was conducted by Rick Doblin in 1986. Rick Doblin founded and became the director of the Multidisciplinary Association for Psychedelic Studies (MAPS). He tracked down nine of the ten students who had taken psilocybin and interviewed seven of them. Remarkably, all of them reported that the experience had changed them in profound ways and had formed the basis for their work and life. This was no small finding. If the effects of a psychedelic experience 30 years ago could be so powerful, there was hope for us all. The experience had not been transitory, but it had resonated with them long thereafter.

He also found some discrepancies with the account that Pahnke had published. Notably, many subjects had struggled with severe anxiety during their experiences. One student had to be restrained and administered Thorazine, which is a powerful antipsychotic, because the student was convinced that he had been chosen to announce the arrival of the Messiah. Therefore, it was clear that there was immense potential to be uncovered, but without the proper conditions, things might go wrong as well. This example refers, again, to the central concepts of "set" and "setting."

Harvard Psilocybin Project

While the Good Friday Experiment introduced us to the psychonaut Walter Panhke, the Harvard Psilocybin Project was the result of two other psychonauts by the names of Timothy Leary and Richard Alpert (later known as Ram Dass). Richard Alpert came to Harvard University in 1953 as an assistant professor after obtaining a PhD in psychology from Stanford University. The early part of his career was concerned with social psychology research. Timothy Leary came to Harvard in 1959 after receiving a PhD in psychology from Berkeley University. His early research focused on social relationships and on the interactions of the various dimensions of personality. Apart from this, he also worked in psychotherapy.

In 1960, Timothy Leary tried magic mushrooms for the first time in Cuernavaca, Mexico. Not long after, he conceived the Harvard Psilocybin Project along with Alpert. They wanted to study the effects of these psychedelics, especially psilocybin, on the human mind and to test whether they had any therapeutic value or not.

In order to convince the university to grant them permission to conduct this experiment, they argued that psychology has a direct connection to and a valid interest in how these psychedelics affect perception, cognition, and emotion in those who ingest them. Remember that, at this time, neither psilocybin nor LSD was illegal, and this was a much easier task to accomplish at that period than it is today.

The aim was to administer psilocybin to volunteer subjects and document its effects on their consciousness in real-time. These experiments ran from 1960 to 1962, when most of the faculty and administration of Harvard started raising concerns about the safety and rigor of their research. Alpert and Leary's colleagues were particularly worried about the poorly controlled conditions of the experiment, non-random selection of the participants, and their unconventional methodologies. The methodology in question was attributable to the two of them reportedly being under the influence of psilocybin themselves while conducting the studies. In fact, editorials in the Harvard Crimson accused both of Alpert and Leary of not only researching the drugs, but also recommending them for recreational use.

While both these researchers defended their experiment and agreed to certain policies to ensure the safety of their volunteers, especially agreeing to not include any undergraduate students in their studies, the experiment was doomed to failure. Initially, they administered psilocybin only to volunteer graduate students, but in 1963, Alpert was fired when he was caught administering psilocybin to an undergraduate outside the university campus. Soon after, Leary was fired as well, and this marked the end of the project.

Facing discreditation and disrepute in the scientific community, due to their poorly conducted experiments, Alpert and Leary's careers in academia were over, but their personal narratives were only just beginning to take shape. In fact, both of them, especially Leary, became poster boys for the counterculture and human potential movement.

Leary, who had long since become disenchanted with the strict nature of scientific protocols and any sort of rules in general, coined the infamous slogan: "Tune in, turn on, drop out." Alpert, on the other hand, took a different route and went to India to study spirituality and wrote the book *Be Here Now* under the name Ram Dass. The book is regarded as a modern spiritual classic.

The Dark Ages: 1970s to 1980s

These experiments and the conditions surrounding them brought to light two terms that had not enjoyed such popularity before. The "counterculture" was a period in the '60s and some part of the '70s which also came to be known pejoratively as "hippie culture." Characterized by the Summer of Love, Woodstock, and the San Francisco acid tests, to name a few, this movement led to widespread use of psychedelics for recreational use. And as the second term, "recreational use," came into focus, it signified the irresponsible and dangerous use of these drugs by youth for no other purposes than to let loose and have fun. Many respected psychonauts frown at the use of this term, and with good reason. Recreation comes from the Latin word *recreare*, which means to create again or renew. It also means mental or spiritual consolation. Therefore, recreational use is not, in its truest sense, the demon that it was meant to be. It's no wonder that the psychonauts place as much importance on the language around these compounds as the compounds themselves. After all, words affect the consciousness too.

It was around this time that there was widespread moral panic among the general public, as well as concerns among members of the scientific community and public policymakers, that psychedelics were leading the country to ruin by targeting its youth. In fact, an appalling footnote to these events was the CIA-sanctioned Project MK-Ultra, which used psychedelics (especially LSD) to control the minds of suspected individuals and force illegal confessions from them. Many illegal experiments were conducted, and while they were officially sanctioned during the year of 1953, by 1967, they had been curtailed. It is a horrifying story that is beyond the scope of this book, but it tells us something about the conditions prevailing at the time.

The two main psychedelics that bore the brunt of this widespread paranoia were LSD and MDMA. The fact that psilocybin carried much less, or almost none, of the countercultural baggage ascribed to LSD served it well when the psychedelic movement saw a renaissance in the late 1990s and early 2000s. On the other hand, LSD became synonymous with the counterculture, and almost any scientist of repute distanced themselves from it. MDMA, which had seen some success in PTSD-related psychotherapy in the 1970s, became known as Ecstasy, a designer drug responsible for fueling club culture and raves.

All these events, together, culminated in Richard Nixon, then the US President, signing the Controlled Substances Act in 1970 and putting most psychedelics on Schedule I. We'll discuss the laws surrounding psychedelics in a later chapter, but for now, let us briefly understand what Schedule I drugs are. According to the US government, any drug or substance that has no Food and Drug Administration (FDA) approved use in the US and has high chances of being abused and causing addiction is known as a Schedule I drug. This means that not only can these drugs not be used by the public, but that all government-sanctioned research around them needs to stop. For many people, this meant no studies, but others faced a more curious phenomenon. While the government forced a lot of studies to close down completely and left the researchers with no choice in the matter, there were a few projects that had the opportunity to run until funding dried up. But lack of funding was not the only issue they faced. The major concern was the possibility of facing ridicule at the hands of others in the scientific community. How could anyone expect themselves to be seen as serious researchers if they were associated with LSD and the like?

Overall, this period can be seen as the "Dark Ages" of psychedelic research. The worst part of this era, according to most psychonauts, was that almost all of the learnings that had been accumulated to date in the field of psychiatry were erased. The psychotherapeutic benefits that had only just begun to be explored were all but forgotten and would remain so for a long time.

The Second Wave: 1990s to Now

I've mentioned before that the history of psychedelics is the history of resurgence, and that is what this period has been about. While most researchers shied away from working on psychedelics after the ban, there was a group of people who led psychedelics from the dark ages to renewed hope. While there were many instances that ignited hope for psychedelics in the 1990s, the core group behind most, if not all, of these developments was known as the Esalen group. The Esalen Institute is a nonprofit American retreat center and community in Big Sur, California, founded in 1962. It is known as the focus of the Human Potential Movement. This movement arose out of the counterculture movement of the 1960s and believed in the concept of extraordinary potential in people that was untapped and needed to be cultivated. And as we all know by now, psychedelics are one of the ways to put the "extra" in extraordinary.

This place would also be remembered for marking the beginning of the next wave of psychedelic research. Some of the prominent figures that made this happen were Roland Griffiths, Bob Schuster, and Bob Jesse.

Council on Spiritual Practices

Some of the psychonauts on this journey were quieter than others, preferring to work behind the scenes if possible. One of them was Rick Doblin, who started MAPS, and the other was Bob Jesse. Jesse was neither a scientist nor a medical professional. He was a vice president at Oracle who wanted to revive psychedelics, not so much for medical purposes, but for spiritual ones. He organized a gathering of researchers and religious figures in order to discuss the spiritual and therapeutic benefits of psychedelics. He was one of the people who preferred the term "entheogens" because he saw these compounds as instrumental in making sacred experiences available to everyone. This was the major aim of the nonprofit group called Council of Spiritual

Practices, which he founded in 1996 and convened at the Esalen Institute.

The group comprised of about 15 people, including "psychedelic elders" such as James Fadiman and Willis Harman, who had conducted early psychedelic research at Stanford University, as well as Huston Smith, the scholar of comparative religion. Intriguingly, Jesse decided to invite a so-called outsider by the name of Bob Schuster, who was a drug-abuse expert and who had recently retired from the National Institute of Drug Abuse (NIDA). Schuster gave them advice on how to go about applying for approvals and also told them to place their bets on psilocybin instead of LSD or MDMA because of its relatively clean image.

It is also interesting to note that the main aim of the group was to conduct respectable research in reputable institutions to gain credibility, but they did not want to do so for clinical purposes. Their aim was to understand spirituality and mystical experiences through the use of these "entheogens." Little did they know that this meeting would set the tone for psychedelic research for years, even in the fields of psychotherapy and psychiatry.

It was after this meeting that Schuster recommended his friend and colleague Roland Griffiths to Bob Jesse. Jesse had been looking for a scientist who was well-regarded and above reproach to give their quest the respectability that it deserved. Griffiths was a scientist who had worked for decades as a drug-addiction researcher at NIDA and held respectable positions in psychiatry and neuroscience at Johns Hopkins University. Hopkins would become the site for this revival as well, and its credibility as a leading institute would bolster the efforts of researchers everywhere. Since Griffiths was seen by everyone who had worked with him, including the director of the National Institute of Mental Health (NIMH), as a scientist who was rigorous in his data analysis, most people were intrigued when he put his weight behind psilocybin.

When Jesse met Griffiths for the first time in Baltimore, they started a series of conversations around spirituality and meditation that resulted in a landmark paper. Griffiths himself had been introduced to Siddha

Yoga in 1994 and had been completely transformed by meditation. At the same time, he was unable to find an outlet to describe his experiences and understanding of the spiritual realm to his colleagues who were scientists. This made his meeting with Jesse all the more serendipitous, and together, they published a paper called "Psilocybin Can Occasion Mystical-Type Experiences Having Substantial and Sustained Personal Meaning and Spiritual Significance" in *Psychopharmacology*.

Paving the Way for Psychedelic Research

The rest, as they say, is history. The impact that the 2006 paper had on the scientific community was something no one had imagined, least of all those involved in its publication. This was the first time, after decades (or maybe ever), that a double-blind, well-controlled study had been conducted at a reputable institute. When the journal invited prominent drug researchers as well as neuroscientists to give their feedback on the study, all of them were hopeful and convinced that this clinical study made a compelling case for serious research around the therapeutic benefits of psychedelics.

A follow-up to this study was conducted in 2011 by Katherine A Maclean along with Griffiths and others to analyze potential changes in personality due to these mystical experiences, and they found a significant increase in "openness" in the participants. More on these two studies will be discussed in the chapter on transcendence.

Along with inquiries into mystical experiences, this paper paved the way for therapeutic research as well. At the University of California, Los Angeles, Charles Grob won FDA approval in 2011 for a Phase I trial to assess the safety, dosing, and efficacy of psilocybin in the treatment of anxiety in cancer patients. In the Phase II trials conducted in 2015 at Hopkins and New York University (NYU), larger groups were involved, and the doses administered were also higher.

Apart from studies that investigated the effects of psilocybin on anxiety of terminal cancer patients, there is an increasing number of studies being conducted in the treatment of addiction, treatment-resistant depression, and other disorders. These studies will be covered in detail in the chapter on psychotherapy using psilocybin and will show how promising the research around this compound is proving to be.

From 1996 to the present, numerous studies have been conducted on the effects of psilocybin on human perception, cognition, and psychopharmacology. Among those are 112 reported studies of psilocybin in humans, including recent therapeutic trials in depression, anxiety, and substance use disorders. With the growing interest in psilocybin, many other FDA-approved clinical trials are underway.

Some researchers have had concerns regarding the safety of administering psilocybin or other psychedelics to patients. Truth is, among the thousands of people who have received psilocybin in clinical trials, there haven't been any reports of psychosis, suicide, or any serious negative effects. This is to be expected because the volunteers in these trials are self-selected, carefully assessed, and prepared well for the treatment beforehand. Even if some participants report feelings of fear or anxiety, they are managed by therapists who are present for this very purpose. In other words, a carefully conducted clinical trial is different from ingesting psychedelics for recreational use, and therefore, the benefits are many, and the risks are almost none.

What Does the Future Hold?

The future holds great promise for clinical research using psilocybin. What's more, the FDA is notably open-minded in its consideration of the subject. In 2018, the FDA granted "breakthrough therapy" status to psilocybin therapy in the still-ongoing clinical trials run by the company Compass Pathways. These trials are investigating psilocybin's potential to treat severe treatment-resistant depression or depression in patients who have not improved after undergoing two different antidepressant treatments.

In 2019, the FDA granted this status to another clinical trial being conducted by the nonprofit Usona Institute. This clinical trial, which includes 80 participants at seven different sites across the U.S., focuses on the efficacy of treating patients with major depressive disorder (MDD) with a single dose of psilocybin.

In the US, almost 17 million people suffer from MDD, which is depression that lasts longer than two weeks. By acknowledging that the treatment of MDD is possible using psilocybin, the FDA has shown faith in the research being conducted. Not only that, but this status of acknowledgment also speeds up the typically sluggish pace of drug development and review. This status is only accorded when preliminary evidence suggests that the drug might be a significant improvement over already available therapy.

We are now at the brink of a new age for psychotherapy, psychiatry, psychopharmacology, and neuroscience.

Chapter 3:

Your Brain on Psilocybin

The next question that arises is: How does psilocybin manage to produce the effects it does on the brain? How does it work immediately after ingestion as well as in the long-term? More importantly, is there a way to understand the working of psilocybin and other psychedelics through neuroscience? While this is a work-in-progress and will be for the near future, there are some exciting developments on the horizon that will help us in understanding how psilocybin affects our brain.

The Chemistry

After ingestion, psilocybin is quickly converted by the body into the pharmacologically active form of psilocin. Psilocin is a tryptamine, much like LSD and 5-MeO-DMT. A tryptamine is a type of organic compound that has two linked rings, one of them containing five atoms and the other containing six. Tryptamines are abundant in nature and function as signaling molecules between cells. Within the human body, serotonin is a famous tryptamine. Serotonin is known chemically as 5-hydroxy-tryptamine. Neurotransmitters like serotonin are the body's chemical messengers. They transmit messages between neurons and from muscles to neurons.

Serotonin binds to many receptors in the brain as well as the body, including the digestive tract. Scientists are still puzzled about many aspects regarding the workings of serotonin. Notably, the effect that serotonin has on neurons depends on the receptor it binds to as well as the location of the receptor. In this way, its action changes completely depending on its context.

All classic psychedelics have a strong affinity with one serotonin receptor known as 5-HT2A. These receptors are abundantly located in the human cortex, which is the most recent and outermost layer of the brain. Since there is a huge similarity between these psychedelics and serotonin, the psychedelics can attach themselves to this receptor site and activate it. This fact was discovered in 1998 by Swiss researcher and psychedelic neuroscience pioneer Franz Vollenweider, who gave his subjects a drug called ketanserin to block this receptor. After this, he administered psilocybin to them and observed that nothing happened. This helped him conclude that psilocybin works by attaching itself to this receptor.

The Phenomenology

Phenomenology is the philosophical study of the structures of experience and consciousness. Why is it relevant in our study of psychedelics? Because there are certain aspects of a psychedelic experience that have confounded many scientists as well as laypeople over the years. After all, psychedelic experiences are unique in that no two experiences are the same. However, the basic themes remain constant. What do I mean by that? Well, when people are in the midst of a journey, their visions are theirs. It could be argued that some visions are the product of suggestions or common myths, but what is more intriguing is that many people report experiences that are distinct but with similar themes. By that I mean that people often talk of "ego-dissolution," or the loss of ego consciousness. Before we try to understand what might occasion this experience, let us understand consciousness as a concept.

Consciousness is something that belongs more to the realm of mysticism than to science, and there are reasons for this. Firstly, we have only just begun to investigate consciousness from a scientific viewpoint. Many scientists believe that consciousness originates in the brain, but not everyone shares this view. If consciousness originates in the brain, then there is hope that, with time and technology, we might be able to understand it better. But what is consciousness in the first place? Is it simply awareness or a fact of being awake? Or is it more than that?

Consciousness arises from the belief that there is an "I" who has subjective experiences. This means that we have a self that experiences different things. It seems like something not up for debate, right? And yet, when people consume psychedelics, this is precisely the kind of thing that gets challenged. By "ego dissolution," we mean that the line between the self and the other, or others, gets blurred. This then leads to another mind-boggling question: Is there even a self, or is it just a construct that gets destroyed when we are having a psychedelic experience?

If this doesn't make you dizzy, I have yet another question for you: What good, if any, does ego dissolution do? And what, if any, are its long-term effects? Oh, and we barely know the answers to any of these questions, least of all if the self, and consequently consciousness, can be proven beyond a doubt.

But psychedelics may help provide some clues in this regard. These compounds produce effects that disrupt what we know as our normal waking consciousness. In contrast to anesthetics, which also cause a disruption to perception, but which shut our systems down, psychedelic experiences are characterized by the ability of the participant to be able to describe what is happening to them in real-time. Another difference between now and the earlier research conducted in this field is that we now have imaging tools available to us that help us correlate these experiences with measures of brain activity. In other words, when I am undergoing "ego dissolution," my brain might show certain activities that can be captured and analyzed to understand the process in real-time. Mind you, the assumption in this methodology is that consciousness lies in the brain.

The Experiments

At the Centre for Psychiatry on the Hammersmith campus of Imperial College in West London, a team comprising David Nutt, a prominent psychopharmacologist, and neuroscientist Robin Carhart-Harris has been working since 2009 on what might be the most exciting neuroscientific study to understand consciousness. They have an ambitious goal in mind: to understand the "neural correlates" of the psychedelic experience. In other words, how does ego dissolution show up as brain activity? They are making this possible using different scanning technologies, including functional magnetic resonance imaging (fMRI) and magnetoencephalography (MEG).

In 2009, the team received approval from the National Health Service (NHS) and the Home Office to study the effects of psilocybin in the brain. Carhart-Harris wanted to volunteer for the study but was dissuaded by Nutt because he was of an anxious disposition and might not have been psychologically suited for the experiment at the time. Also, they didn't want to risk influencing the objectivity of the studies by becoming a subject. When a colleague volunteered to have psilocybin injected in him and have his brain studied, the experiment was underway.

Since a lot of the experience of being on a psychedelic might seem like a dream (even though people report seeing things more clearly than they ever have in their lives), the scientists expected that there would be increased activity, characterized by increased blood flow, in the emotional centers of the brain. Vollenweider had published data that indicated that psychedelics increased brain activity in the frontal lobes, which are responsible for cognition and other executive functions like memory, flexible thinking, and self-control. They thought that the results would be a version of the dreaming brain, but, instead, they were in for a shock.

Initial data showed that psilocybin causes decrease in blood flow, and hence, brain activity, in certain areas. To confirm whether they were right, they used a second measure that looked at changes in oxygen consumption to measure elevated brain activity. The data was conclusive: psilocybin did cause a decrease in brain activity, specifically in an area known as the Default Mode Network (DMN).

Default Mode Network and Psilocybin

This part of the brain has only been known to neuroscience in the last couple of decades. In 2001, Marcus Raichle, a neurologist at Washington University School of Medicine in St. Louis, MO, published a landmark paper in *Proceedings of the National Academy of Sciences in the United States of America (PNAS)* called "A Default Mode of Brain Function." In this paper, he explained how he had discovered this region of the brain.

While his subjects were awaiting their tests and had their brains hooked on to the scanning technology, Raichle noticed that, while their brains were at rest, there was increased activity in a certain region. When the brain was not involved in any activity or didn't have any demands on its attention, this area showed heightened activity, which initially seemed counterintuitive.

Truth is, when a person is not involved with the outer world, their brains are not dormant. In fact, this is a period in which the person engages in "metacognitive" processes like mental time travel, mental constructions such as the self or ego, and self-reflection, to name a few. These are processes that can be extrapolated to be seen as the evidence of consciousness. Therefore, it makes sense to believe that the clues to consciousness might lie in these regions of the brain. The other way in which DMN is significant is because it is known as the "orchestra conductor" of the brain. To understand this function better, we need to understand how the brain works. There are many regions of the brain that have distinct functions. Those that are known as "higher-level" functions, which are associated with the cortex, such as thought and perception, suppress the lower-level functions such as emotion and memory.

This hierarchy is important because it keeps the brain from descending into chaos. The DMN is responsible for keeping the different regions from interacting with each other all the time and for giving precedence to certain functions over others. The DMN is also called "the me network" because it is important in the construction of the ego. It is also known to contain the autobiographical material by which we tell the story of our lives.

While it seems to have a lot of evolutionary benefits, many scientists have speculated if it isn't also the cause of many problems and disorders in adults (DMN is not active in children until much later stages of their development). What are the issues around heightened activity in the DMN, and how can psychedelics counter those issues?

A 2010 paper published in *Science* was titled "A Wandering Mind is an Unhappy Mind" and discussed whether higher levels of self-reflection helped us or not. While self-reflection and related activities seem to contribute to higher intellectual development and more accomplishments, they also perpetuate a feeling of being separate from nature and others. In other words, the greater the ego, the less the feeling of connectedness with the universe, which leads to greater unhappiness. How so? According to Carhart-Harris, the DMN imposes order on the brain, and excess order leads to depression, addiction, and other mood disorders. Let that sink in.

There is another aspect of the brain that we rely on as adults trying to navigate this chaotic world. The brain engages in what is known as "predictive coding." This is a phenomenon present in the adult brain. The brain is a complex organ, and to minimize the complexity and uncertainty of our daily lives, it tries to help us by making calculated guesses about the world, like Google does when doing a search. This means that our experiences inform our thinking process and help us in not having to think deeply each time we need to perform repetitive or familiar tasks. The brain becomes better at this with experience. We can see why this is advantageous to us, but the disadvantages are not as clearly understood.

Predictive coding ensures that we become set in our ways pretty soon and form habits that usually last us the rest of our lives. As adults, the same order that keeps us sane and functional in this world might also lead to depression and lack of wonder.

When Carhart-Harris published the results of his study on psilocybin on the brain in a 2012 paper in *PNAS*, he was contacted by Judson Brewer, who was a researcher at Yale using fMRI scans to study the brains of experienced meditators. According to him, Carhart-Harris' scans were remarkably like the ones Brewer had seen in the meditators.

Meditation is another method used by many to achieve a transcendence of the self. Since the effect is similar to that of the ego dissolution produced by psilocybin, the scans registered a similar decrease in activity in the DMN. Therefore, different techniques such as holotropic breathing, sensory deprivation, meditation, psychedelic experiences, and experiences of awe all lead to this phenomenon in the brain. What does this mean for us in terms of our processes as well as our lives?

The Impact

What exactly causes this decreased activity in the DMN is still unclear, though some researchers think it might be due to reduced blood flow to the receptors in the cortex. There are certain effects of this reduced activity that are of note, however. For one, when the DMN becomes less active, our sense of self starts to dissolve. This means that we feel as if we are boundaryless, and that there is no distinction between us and anything else in the world or beyond. R. Gordon Wasson said, loosely paraphrasing William Blake, "The mushroom permits you to see, more clearly than our perishing mortal eye can see, vistas beyond the horizons of this life, to travel backwards and forwards in time, to enter other planes of existence, even (as the Indians say) to know God." Indeed, this is a description that is all too common in psychedelic experiences. This gives rise to experiences that are out of the ordinary, yes, but they also make these experiences seem true and objective rather than subjective. Without an "I" to witness the event, the event ceases to be specific to the self and thus becomes objective. This is what is known as the "noetic quality" of a mystical experience. This is also what makes the participants of such experiences absolutely sure of what they saw and their affirmations that they saw the truth and nothing else.

Apart from this, when the DMN is unable to control the various regions of the brain and assign them hierarchies, the lower-order functions suddenly become much more significant than earlier. This means that your emotions and memory take precedence over cognition and related functions. What does this mean? During a psychedelic experience, you are more susceptible to flashbacks, childhood memories including trauma, and the like. Everything that is suppressed by your brain in the normal state comes to the surface.

Since the DMN keeps the various regions of the brain from interacting with each other, a psychedelic experience has the opposite effect. It allows the various regions like memory and emotion to interact with visual and auditory processing centers. Not only that, it allows us to take in more of the outside world than usual. This is a bottom-up approach where the senses take precedence over the higher-order functions. Scientists still face the dilemma of determining whether the brain on psychedelics prefers a top-down or the bottom-up approach to dealing with data. But one thing is for sure. In this state, there is a lot of "cross talk" and mixing of signals between the different regions of the brain. Is this good or bad? The answer, as with most things, is that…it depends.

The Potential

According to some scientists, including Carhart-Harris, the primitive brain was more prone to "magical thinking." In this brain, there was room for intense and often wild imagination as well as superstitious beliefs. It wasn't a practical or an evolutionarily fit brain. He also believes that, when we consume psychedelics, our brains revert to this primitive state. It is certainly a valid argument. But is it all bad? After all, many scientists, Carhart-Harris included, have also asked the question, "Is the price for having a strong sense of self not reduced happiness and creativity?"

As mentioned earlier, our brains are wired to think of an increase in randomness or uncertainty as a sign of trouble. Of course, this is a spectrum, and on one hand we have highly ordered or structured states, while on the other we have highly disordered or chaotic states. In the high-disordered states, such as those experienced through ingesting psychedelics, we have too much information flowing inside our brains. Our sense of self is corroded, and our usual processes are also confused. This may be why many people are able to notice things that they didn't earlier, have visions of their past, see people from their childhood, and even experience synesthesia. For example, a colorblind person might be able to see colors, or a person might be able to smell blue because his emotion, memory, and sensory perception is now linked to auditory and visual processing systems. At the same time, having a lot of information coming at us in unusual ways also leads us to form connections and see patterns that we couldn't see earlier. What do we mean by lateral thinking or creative processes? Essentially, these processes arise out of thinking in a way that is not normal to us. There is a lot of so-called useless data coming at us, but some of it might be truly transformational.

The ordered or structured states are related to a stronger sense of self and a surer way of navigating the world. But they are also related to excessive rumination, which in turn has been linked to depression, anxiety, and addiction. At the same time, having a sense of self that seems inflexible and unquestionable leaves us closed to wonder. Therefore, when people are on psychedelics, they notice the intense green of the trees as if for the first time. They also notice patterns in music, art, and nature that they couldn't have noticed otherwise. A greater appreciation of the world we live in and a sense of wonder keeps us alive. At the same time, a stronger sense of self means a greater separateness from nature. The less we are connected to nature, the more we are susceptible to feeling lonely and depressed.

The truth is, too much randomness is certainly unhelpful because it may lead to magical thinking and even psychosis, but too little of it is not helpful either. This is why understanding how psilocybin (and later LSD) affects the DMN gives hope for the use of these psychedelics in helping both mentally healthy and mentally ill patients. In mentally healthy patients, psychedelics might help in shaking off the old patterns of thought and behavior which keep us from being innovative, creative, and passionate about life. As Carhart-Harris points out: Taking psychedelics is like "shaking the snow globe", it disrupts these patterns and explodes cognitive barriers. In fact, microdosing psilocybin may lead to better problem solving as well, as has been explored in a 2019 study published by James Fadiman in the *Journal of Psychoactive Drugs*.

In mentally ill patients, this research provides hope in the treatment of treatment-resistant depression and other mood disorders that might be a result of excessive activity in the DMN.

Neuroplasticity

Another major question that most researchers want the answer to is: Are the effects of psychedelics, like psilocybin, on the brain long-lasting? If we have a chance to see things from a new perspective, be more creative, experience less depression, and so on, wouldn't we want the effects to be persistent? And do the drugs themselves lead to this persistence?

Vollenweider has suggested that the psychedelic experience in and of itself may lead to neuroplasticity, which is a state in which the brain is more susceptible to changing its thought and behavior patterns. Notably, meditation is supposed to increase neuroplasticity in the brain as well. Others, like Carhart-Harris, think that even a temporary resetting of the brain might be useful in disrupting unhealthy patterns of thinking and allow for healthier patterns to form during the space in which our normal consciousness isn't working normally.

While there is still much research to be done in this field, there is hope that these experiences can change our neural pathways permanently, and for the better.

Chapter 4:

Psychonauts: Pioneers of a Brave New World

Throughout this book, we've encountered many psychonauts like Maria Sabina, Gordon Wasson, Richard Alpert, Timothy Leary, Bob Jesse, Roland Griffiths, and so on. This chapter is dedicated solely to some more psychonauts who have made it possible for the psychedelic revolution to happen. They belong to different eras, and some of them have lived through the different waves of psychedelic research. They have all come to this experience from different points of view and varied beliefs, but all of them are crucial to the story of psychedelics. In fact, their lives contain lessons not only for those who are interested in the therapeutic and transcendental effects of these compounds, but for anyone who is interested in exploring new and varied states of being—including artists, scientists, philosophers, and so on.

Aldous Huxley: Opening the Doors of Perception

No discussion of psychonauts can be complete without discussing the extraordinary life, and death, of Aldous Huxley. He is known as an author of groundbreaking work and equally revolutionary ideas, but curiously enough, he didn't think that the only purpose of taking psychedelics was to become a better writer or to be more creative.

According to legend, Huxley was first introduced to psychedelics when he was given mescaline by the famous occultist Aleister Crowley. In the 1930s, before taking mescaline, he had authored the novel *Brave New World*, which described the use of psychotropic substances for mind control in a subservient population. The irony is not lost on anyone.

After having experienced mescaline, he wrote about the experiences and his ideas in his 1953 book called *The Doors of Perception.* Anyone who has ever been interested in or involved in the history of psychedelics has read this book. (The rock group The Doors, and its leader, Jim Morrison, who was open to experiencing peyote, were allegedly inspired so much by this work that they named their band after its title). Interestingly, Huxley said that he did not witness any visions while on mescaline, as is expected by most people. In fact, what he did witness was a subtle but real shift in consciousness, a feeling of transcendence – and you guessed it: ego-dissolution. He felt indistinguishable from and united with the Ultimate Being.

Remember Humphry Osmond and the coining of the term "psychedelics"? It was Huxley who gave him the original term after ingesting LSD. In fact, Huxley didn't believe in or support the use of these substances for recreational purposes as had become the norm in the sixties. He believed that the proper use of these substances could lead to enlightenment, self-discovery, and an expansion of the consciousness, as well as effect great political change. He talked about these ideas in his final utopian novel *Island*, which was published in 1962.

When asked about the effect of psychedelics on creativity, he explained that, while the experience could help anyone, including an artist, see the world in a different and entirely new way, no one should take psychedelics only so that they could write a bestseller. There were two reasons for this notion. One, a psychedelic experience cannot be dictated beforehand. This is true even now, after the understanding of "set" and "setting." We must remember that Huxley took these psychedelics without any supervision or controlled setting. Therefore, he felt even more deeply that one doesn't know what to expect in this scenario. Two, even if you did get some amazing new insights that could form the basis of your newest work, why would you want to do that instead of simply taking in the whole experience fully? This certainly makes sense. He also believed that the kind of experience he was talking about made it nearly impossible to be captured in words.

Another belief of Huxley's was the effects of an experience outlasted the experience itself. Even if someone did not have access to all their memories and so-called visions after the experience, they could still feel themselves changed after having experienced diverse worlds and the worlds of other visionaries. They could carry the remnants of this transformation and use it to understand themselves better overall. Even though there wasn't much in the way of psychotherapy using psychedelics, at least in a controlled manner, during his time, he hinted at their use for dealing with trauma. He believed that psychedelic trips "helped in bringing back a lot of buried material." Thus, what would be achieved in years of psychoanalysis, could be achieved in hours, and more powerfully so, through the correct use of psychedelics.

His ideas during his lifetime were certainly radical, but his death was even more so. It was also one of the first recorded experiences of dealing with cancer-related death using psychedelics. When Huxley was diagnosed with terminal cancer, he initially had trouble accepting the fact of his impending death. His wife, Laura, who was beside him on this entire journey, tried to guide him using Tim Leary, Richard Alpert (Ram Dass), and Ralph Metzner's manual extracted from their book, *The Psychedelic Experience*, based upon the Tibetan *Book of the Dead.* Huxley, however, reminded her that this guide was used to help people come back from their psychedelic experiences and reintegrate with their lives. He didn't believe that it would help someone having to deal with the scary proposition of facing death.

Laura consulted with Sidney Cohen, who was then a leading psychiatrist working with LSD. Cohen had conducted early LSD research in the 1950s and was a noted US public expert on drug abuse from the 1960s to the 1980s. Not only was he a Professor of Psychiatry at the University of California, Los Angeles (UCLA), but he also served in the Nixon administration as the first Director in the Division of Narcotic Abuse and Drug Addiction at the National Institute of Mental

Health (NIMH). During this time, he also authored more than 250 articles and books, including *The Beyond Within: The LSD Story*.

Cohen told Laura that he had used LSD to help two terminal cancer patients come to terms with their diagnosis. In one patient, there had been a graceful acceptance of death, while another remained unaffected. This was before any large clinically approved trials were underway on this subject.

Eventually, Huxley asked her to inject him with 100 micrograms of LSD on his deathbed. She did so after taking some herself, and then guided him peacefully in his final moments. Those that witnessed the scene vowed that they had never seen such a peaceful transition in someone with Huxley's physical condition. While no one could know for sure what was going on inside his mind in those final hours, it seemed like a peaceful death for others.

This was an extraordinary man who believed that all of humankind benefited from knowing that there were other worlds out there, different from the one we live in and take for granted. If we can take anything from him, it should be this outlook, especially in a world where fossilized views have become the norm.

Alfred Hubbard: The Captain Trips of America

One might argue that few figures in the history of the psychedelic movement were as influential as Timothy Leary. While his efforts cannot be discounted, it is also true that many other highly influential figures worked quietly behind the scenes and revolutionized the landscape way before the hullabaloo surrounding Leary and his associates.

Alfred Hubbard was one such visionary, though he would be uncomfortable about being called that. Way before LSD became wildly popular among the masses and then demonized due to the counterculture, Hubbard explored its clinical uses and introduced them to countless others (though not in the way that Leary did).

Though relatively little is known about him in his early days, he is said to have been born in Kentucky around the turn of the 20th century. He was always ingenious and used his intellect and interest in engineering to explore nuclear energy, even patenting some dubious technology that was later termed as a hoax. His life, before discovering LSD, was also colorful, to say the least. He is said to have been involved with the infamous Olmstead bootlegging operation. According to some sources, he was responsible for maintaining the fleet of ships that were essential to Roy Olmstead's bootlegging operation. In this process, he also started Seattle's first radio station. Later, when the authorities got suspicious of his involvement in the operation, he is said to have made a deal with them and then played both parties against each other for some time before being caught. This was the beginning of a strange and interesting relationship with law enforcement officials that would last his entire life. Just after World War II ended, he started a company with his wife to market radioactive materials. This venture failed, but it had been established that Hubbard was no ordinary man.

His life changed in 1951 when he heard about and then ingested LSD. The experience was truly transformative and revelatory for him, as he reportedly witnessed events as incredible and profound as his own conception, time on a cosmic scale, and the beginning of creation itself. The effects were profound, to say the least. This is when he found his true calling in life.

The money he had made through his patents and other illicit activities, as well as the government and business connections he enjoyed, allowed him to obtain a massive dose of LSD directly from Sandoz Pharmaceuticals. Though the exact volume is debated, some records show six thousand vials, and still others say it was closer to a liter. Some even say it was forty-three cases that were either kept in a bank vault in Zurich or buried in Death Valley. The point is that he had more LSD than any other entity, excluding Sandoz, in the US. He apparently carried vials of this drug in a leather satchel with plans to "liberate human consciousness." He collaborated with Humphry

Osmond and is said to have influenced 6,000 people, including Myron Stolaroff, an early figure in Silicon Valley who would then introduce Steve Jobs to the psychedelic.

There are many things of note about Hubbard's involvement with the psychedelic movement. Though he, too, like Leary, believed in the consciousness-expanding effects of psychedelics, he also thought it was important to change the minds of influential people before reaching the masses. Unlike Leary, he didn't distribute LSD to the masses but focused on taking a top-down approach by reaching out to influential political, medical, and cultural figures.

Another important contribution he made is still recognized in the field of psychotherapy. Known as the "Hubbard Room," this was a result of his understanding that the mind on LSD might not feel comfortable in sterile hospital settings and that relaxing the patient was important. Knowingly or not, he understood the importance of "setting" way before it became a buzzword in psychedelics. This led him to create a room that had soft lighting, soft pillows, calming music, and so on. He also understood that the mind goes in various directions on a psychedelic journey and tried to influence the direction taken by patients based on what he thought they needed most. For example, if someone needed to become more open and relaxed, he would ask them to look at an image of a melting glacier. On the other hand, if someone was looking to have a mystical experience involving Jesus, he would ask them to look at the picture before beginning the experience. These ideas were quite revolutionary at the time. In fact, Hubbard passionately believed that psychedelics should be taken in controlled settings in the presence of trained professionals to be able to take safe and effective journeys. At the same time, he was more content simply providing the means necessary for the experience and letting people discover the journey themselves.

Despite Hubbard's past, he managed to enjoy the government's support on various occasions. When he was able to secure an Investigational New Drug Permit from the FDA, he got together with Humphry Osmond and Canadian psychiatrist Abram Hoffer to pioneer an LSD-assisted therapy for alcohol addicts. The recovery rate of patients was said to be around 60-70%, far above that of Alcoholics Anonymous at the time. Instead of using "aversion therapy," he gave the patients a dose of liquid LSD that allowed them to gain a new perspective on their destructive habits. He was also well-respected as a therapist during these journeys with patients.

The counterculture movement, which launched the public careers of his peers like Alpert and Leary, was what eventually led to the end of his quest to bring the therapeutic possibilities of psychedelics to life. After LSD use was criminalized, he lost a lot of money on the vials that he had bought. He tried getting institutes to allow the use of psychedelics for cancer therapy but failed. Eventually, he was recruited by Willis Harman, who was then the director of the Educational Policy Research Center within the Stanford Research Institute (SRI) of Stanford University. Here he was assigned to the Alternative Futures Project in which he ran the LSD sessions as a part of future-oriented strategic planning for corporations and government agencies. Harman shared Hubbard's vision of introducing LSD to political and intellectual leaders of the world.

While Hubbard died in 1982, well before he could witness the second wave of psychedelic research, he was clearly ahead of his time, and modern psychedelic research owes him a lot, not least of all his efforts in bringing respectability to the field.

Ralph Metzner: The Student Who Became the Teacher

The Harvard Psilocybin Project brought to the fore two psychonauts, Timothy Leary and Richard Alpert. A third figure who was introduced to psilocybin through the project was Ralph Metzner, a respected figure in the history of psychedelics.

He was born in Berlin and moved to the United Kingdom (UK) after World War II. There he studied philosophy and political science at

Oxford before coming to Harvard in 1958 to study psychology at a graduate level. He learned behaviorist learning theory and psychoanalysis at Harvard before encountering the Harvard Psilocybin Project.

As part of the volunteer program, he had his first experience with psilocybin in March 1961, and he was always deeply grateful to Harvard for introducing him to the field of psychedelics through that experience. Around this time, concerns had started mounting regarding the unscientific and unconventional methods of the two researchers, and graduate students were prohibited from using psilocybin-related research in their doctoral dissertations. He completed his dissertation in another project and received a doctorate in clinical psychology. Later he also completed a NIMH postdoctoral fellowship in psychopharmacology at Harvard Medical School.

When Alpert and Leary were fired from the project, Metzner moved to a communal living setting in New York, where they continued their research on psychedelics and consciousness. By this time, psilocybin had become increasingly difficult to source, so their sessions mostly focused on LSD.

It was here that Metzner wrote his first book in collaboration with Leary and Alpert. As mentioned earlier, this book, known as *The Psychedelic Experience: A Manuel Based on The Tibetan Book of the Dead* was published in 1964 and was based on a translation of Tibetan texts. This was the same book that Laura Huxley used to guide her husband during his final days. While the original texts were a guide to negotiating the intermediate state (*bardo*) between one life and the next, Metzner and the others reformulated the prayers.

In their book, they used the reformulated text to guide people on their psychedelic journeys as they moved from one state of consciousness to the next. It was a practice deeply rooted in spirituality and an understanding of the different kinds of mystical experiences.

When the three men went their separate ways, Leary becoming a vocal proponent of the counterculture and Alpert trying to find spiritual growth in India, Metzner continued to stay in academia. He edited the publication started by them, known as *The Psychedelic Review,* and then worked as a clinical psychologist in California.

Throughout his life, he published various essays and around 20 books. In 1968, he published *The Ecstatic Adventure*, an edited collection of essays that explored the psychological and societal impact of psychedelics. His 1971 work, called *Maps of Consciousness*, investigated many esoteric traditions, and hoped to encourage readers to explore consciousness deeply.

In 1975, he became a professor at the California Institute of Asian Studies (CIAS), which is now known as the California Institute of Integral Studies (CIIS). Today, this institute is at the forefront of psychology graduate training programs and conducts research in areas that explore the human consciousness. Ralph taught here for three decades and during this time also researched, wrote, and taught seminars. He also maintained a psychotherapy practice till his last days. His last book was published in 2018, weeks before his death, and was called *Searching for the Philosopher's Stone: Encounters with Mystics, Scientists, and Healers.* In this book, he described his relationship with, and expressed gratitude towards, all the teachers in his life.

His life was marked by respect for various spiritual traditions in the world. He tried to draw from the teachings of ancient European as well as Eastern traditions and use them to explore consciousness. He also believed that understanding consciousness through psychedelics and other means might be key to reducing the suffering of people, a belief that fueled his psychotherapy practice.

Stanislav Grof: From Psychedelics to Holotropic Breathwork

Stanislav Grof is one of the most respected psychiatrists in the world. He has dedicated himself to understanding and exploring the human consciousness and facilitating healing through these journeys. Not only has he expanded the field of psychedelic-assisted research but has also developed new tools to help people heal.

While studying medicine, he naturally gravitated towards psychiatry and Freudian psychoanalysis. During his PhD in Prague, Czechoslovakia became a hub of psychedelic research, which piqued his curiosity. Along with his colleagues, he ran several sessions in the 1960s looking into the effects of LSD and DMT on individuals. What fascinated him was the potential these compounds held in exploring and affecting the human consciousness. Giving small doses of LSD could make people enter deep states of consciousness and then return to normal states while apparently being altered forever at a deeper level.

These experiments made him believe that psychedelics were as important to the field of psychiatry as the telescope and microscope were in their respective fields. This is because both these instruments served as the amplifier of things placed in their field of vision. In the same way, psychedelics had the ability to amplify the mental processes present in the brain which were not visible in a normal state of consciousness.

As someone deeply interested in psychoanalysis, he saw psychedelics as a way to fully understand the subconscious using scientific methods. Before the ban on psychedelics in the US, Grof spent 14 years conducting psychedelic research in the US and Czechoslovakia. He was a pioneer in psychotherapy using psychedelics, having spent seven years in Czechoslovakia conducting two LSD sessions per day and then moving to the US to work at esteemed institutions like Johns Hopkins University and Maryland Psychiatric Research Center.

The psychotherapy sessions conducted by Grof are thought by many to be the gold standard in psychedelic research. He conducted almost 4,500 sessions, and his goal was to assist the patient on his journey by making space for them and allowing them to discover themselves on their own. He made sure he was present with them and tried to make the atmosphere as hospitable as possible. He specifically used eye shades and calming music to help the patients feel relaxed and confident in undertaking the journey. He believes that these methods accelerated the therapeutic effects of such sessions.

When the US banned all research and use of psychedelics, he was understandably disappointed. He believed that, by abandoning research on such promising substances, not only were they giving up on understanding the drugs and their effects better, but they were also giving up on some of the promising methods of understanding the human mind and consciousness at a much deeper level.

As someone who had been so deeply entrenched in the ways of working with psychedelics and having witnessed the effects on his patients beforehand, Grof didn't feel like going back to other tools which he felt by now were primitive compared to the ones he had been using. This is why he became a scholar-in-residence at the famed Esalen Institute in 1973 and discovered a new tool called Holotropic Breathwork along with his wife.

Holotropic comes from the Greek and literally translates to "moving towards wholeness." This process is a combination of breathing, evocative music, and other forms of sound, bodywork, and artistic expression. According to Grof, this method has tremendous potential, much like psychedelics, to help individuals explore their inner selves and consciousness and use it to fulfil their own potential.

The method is evocative of the psychedelic sessions that Grof was known for conducting. The "breather" is asked to lie down on a mat with eye shades on while music plays in the background. Much like therapists, "sitters" are present to hold space for the breathers and to guide them along if needed. The sessions usually end with discussion and drawing, to help them communicate their experiences in a way that suits them.

While there has been little clinical research done on Holotropic Breathwork as of now, there are discussions around it, like those explored with psychedelics and meditation, in their effect on the human consciousness. Remember our discussion on the Default Mode Network? It is believed that Holotropic Breathwork can also be used to see similar results in the DMN and help patients in various ways. Since the psychedelic movement is seeing a renaissance of sorts, and Grof is an established authority in the field, one can hope that there will be more research on this relatively new and exciting field as well.

Currently, both Grof and his wife alternate between the US and Germany and spend most of their time traveling to teach the Holotropic Breathwork technique to practitioners, as well as patients, all over the world.

While his techniques might have changed, Grof remains committed to his original vision: To help people understand themselves and gain from the therapeutic benefits of psychedelics as well as other modes of alternative therapy.

William A. Richards: The Man Who Has Seen It All

William Richards is another giant of the psychedelic movement and someone who has been a part of it for over five decades now and still going strong. This is no mean feat. Richards is an ordained minister (though he never pastored a church) with advanced degrees from Yale Divinity School and Andover-Newton Theological School. He is also a researcher at the Johns Hopkins Center for Psychedelic & Consciousness Research and has helmed many studies around psychedelics for decades. Not only has he been involved in investigating how transcendence can lead to a better quality of life, as well as death, but he has also looked at the effects of psychedelics on mental disorders. His life has prepared him for this unique mix of science and the sacred.

When he was a 23-year-old theology student in Gottingen, Germany, he first tried psilocybin. This was in 1963. As it turns out, the experience transformed him completely and set the course for the rest of his life. That first trip gave him a sense of awareness of beauty and love that he had not known until then. Not only that, the trip helped him in developing self-confidence and experiencing a reduction in anxiety. He felt at peace with himself and understood the importance of genuine connections. These are all huge things to experience after one trip, but that has been the case for so many people.

After this experience, he set out on a lifelong journey to understand psychedelics and the various kinds of religious experiences. Having been influenced by and worked with many other psychonauts during his lifetime, he has a wealth of knowledge, as well as the kind of wisdom that only comes from a lifetime of incredible experiences. He also started this journey at an opportune moment, for in the 1960s, psychedelics were still legal and were also being widely researched.

He studied with Abraham Maslow, the legendary psychologist. He visited Timothy Leary, Richard Alpert, and Ralph Metzner in Millbrook, New York. He was a part of many pioneering studies in psychedelic-assisted psychotherapy in Maryland. Here, he worked with both Walter Pahnke and Stanislav Grof and administered LSD to hundreds of patients. He studied the effects of the psychedelics on conditions like alcohol and heroin addiction, schizophrenia, and existential distress in terminally ill cancer patients. At the same time, he explored the various religions of the world, visited religious sites, and started meditating.

In his 2015 book *Sacred Knowledge: Psychedelics and Religious Experiences*, he details all these experiences and makes a point that, if psychedelics are used in a safe manner, they can not only help in alleviating mental health-related issues such as addiction, depression, and anxiety, but can also accelerate the spiritual growth and general wellbeing of otherwise healthy people. This is an important factor for him. He believes that anyone can benefit from these compounds and expand their consciousness to live more creatively and fully. In fact, he organized a recently concluded FDA-approved study at Johns Hopkins in 2015 to examine the effects of psilocybin-facilitated experiences on the psychology and effectiveness of religious professionals. The aim of this study was to understand how mystical experiences lead to feelings of awe and how these feelings lead to changes in the behavior of those that experience them while also improving their quality of life and relationships. Many of the volunteers who participated, most of whom were religious professionals, came away with an overwhelmingly positive experience that made them believe in the amazing benefits of using psychedelics in safe and supportive environments. Richards is hopeful that we may still see the day when the government allows the use of psychedelics at religious centers in the presence of trained medical and religious professionals.

When Richards completed his psychiatry training in the 2000s, he was introduced to selective serotonin reuptake inhibitors (SSRIs) as well as cognitive behavioral therapy (CBT) as tools for psychotherapy. As it turns out, he felt dejected by their effects (or lack thereof) and quit psychiatry as a result. It was only after he started conducting research around psychedelics, including MDMA, that he felt there was renewed hope for psychotherapy using psychedelics. He is one of the world's leading proponents of psychedelic-assisted psychotherapy.

According to Richards, some of the most meaningful work he has done has been in end-of-life care of patients suffering from terminal cancer. He believes that psychedelics can help immensely in bringing peace and joy to patients during their last months, especially improving their relationships with their loved ones. This is the work that he plans to build on with his son Brian, who is also a clinical psychologist. His aim is to open an oncology center where patients can receive therapy along with psychedelics. He is most excited about the prospect that oncology centers might include psilocybin-based studies in the future.

As someone who has worked in psychotherapy for decades, these new developments are related to two important aspects of this journey. For one, he firmly believes that psychonauts and other researchers in the field, as well as those who support psychedelics in general, should be careful about treating their detractors with respect. Having experienced the paranoia of the seventies, he is keen on it not being repeated. He believes that the attitudes of those involved with the counterculture were as much to blame for the ban as were any legitimate concerns around the usage of the drugs. Deference to people in authority seems to be key in ensuring that the psychedelic renaissance does not end abruptly.

Secondly, with the increasing instances of psychedelic-assisted psychotherapy, the question of training therapists effectively becomes paramount. He offers advice regarding this as well. The man who has written the "flight instructions" for psychedelic journeys believes that it is the presence of the guide that is more important than the quality of the guide. The most important factor in making sure that the patient is safe and has a good journey is an establishment of trust. The therapist should be able to convey to the patient a sense of openness that makes the patient trust them. They should also understand that no two experiences will be the same and different patients might experience different kinds of journeys. As long as the patient feels safe, they should be able to have transforming experiences that will serve them beyond the sessions.

Richards is still actively involved in many studies in numerous institutions, and his life evokes both a passion for his work as well as compassion for those he wants to serve through this work. In other words, he makes science seem sacred.

This is by no means a comprehensive list of the amazing pioneers who have dedicated themselves to this field of research and inquiry, but it hopefully gives you a glimpse of the work that has been going on behind the scenes to make a future like ours possible.

Chapter 5:

Healing: We Need to Talk About Psychedelic-Assisted Psychotherapy

The next two chapters will deal exclusively with the impact of psychedelics on psychotherapy. Remember the "breakthrough therapy" status awarded to psilocybin in two recent instances? There is a lot going on in the world of psychedelic-assisted psychotherapy that is a cause of hope for many people who have been suffering in silence for years. In this chapter, we will talk about the conventional tools of psychotherapy and their constraints. We will also discuss the reasons behind favoring psychedelics as tools for psychotherapy and why they work so well.

Why Has It Taken So Long?

First, let us address the elephant in the room. If psychedelics are so powerful in the treatment of numerous mental health disorders, why have they not enjoyed greater support? Well, there is, of course, the dubious perception of these drugs created by their Schedule I drug status, the government and media propaganda. Scientists, health professionals and policy makers need to be reeducated on the benefits of psychedelics. It has taken a long time to convince the policy makers to even allow studies to be conducted in these fields. What are the specific concerns, and how valid are they?

The initial concerns have been focused on whether the trials are randomized and effectively controlled. Most of the trials conducted today adhere to these methods. What about their being blind? Truth is, in psychedelic-assisted psychotherapy, it is easy for patients to figure out if they were given a drug or a placebo. But more importantly, there are two aspects of the experience that have made many researchers question the true efficacy of these drugs.

As we all know, science is not fond of anecdotal reports. In fact, in order to give credence to any study, it is necessary to vary only one variable at a time, keeping the others constant, and then measuring the impact of the change in this variable. In the psychedelic experience, this is more complicated than it seems.

Set and Setting

Let us understand the concept of "set" and "setting" in psychedelic-assisted psychotherapy. One of the major reasons why the same medicine has different effects on different patients (thus making the tests seem unreliable) is that the effects of the medicine depend on the set of the person. Set refers to the personality, preparation, expectation (or mindset), and intention of the person having the experience. Add to that is the effect of setting, which implies that the physical, social, and cultural environment in which the experience takes place is equally important. This means that, if the patient is already susceptible to anxiety, it is much more likely that they will have an episode of anxiety during the treatment. On the other hand, if they feel adequately prepared for the journey they are undertaking, they can be expected to have a calmer and more fruitful experience. In the same way, if the substances are taken in uncontrolled conditions in an irresponsible manner, there is a greater likelihood of experiencing what is known as a "bad" trip. This is also why therapists have been stressing both preparation as well as an appropriate environment, setting, to ensure their patients have better outcomes.

There are two important factors to consider here. For one, set and setting influences not just psychedelics, but, also, many other medicines which work on influencing mood and behavior. Secondly, set and setting are crucial to the impact that these medicines have on treating disorders. This is especially seen in studies that examine transcendence through these experiences. Of course, it also makes the experience highly subjective. Add to that the irrational optimism that some researchers have regarding the benefits of these compounds, and you can understand where the trepidation stems from.

Another important factor that we've discussed in some detail in the third chapter is that most of the benefits we see in these studies are supposedly a result of transcendence of the ego. Again, this is a highly subjective experience and difficult to quantify in any way. When we want to examine the causes behind the spectacular results that we are seeing, it is natural to balk at the suggestion that everything lies in the consciousness and its subsequent dissolution.

That being said, two things are irrefutable. One, that recent studies have shown tremendous promise in psychotherapy, and the government, as well as mental health professionals, have finally begun to take serious notice. Secondly, neuroscience research is beginning to probe deeper into why these compounds work where most others have failed. We might finally be getting some answers. Before we delve deep into these studies and their results, let us understand what the old tools of psychotherapy are and why they prove to be ineffective in many instances.

Mental Health and Old Tools of Psychotherapy

According to the Centers for Disease Control and Prevention, almost one in five adults in the US experiences a mental health condition in any given year. Even children are falling prey to these conditions, most notably, states of anxiety and depression. What are some of the common afflictions that affect us today? These disorders include anxiety, depression, panic disorders, PTSD, addictions, including alcohol and tobacco, OCD, and eating disorders. The intensity of these disorders varies from individual to individual, but there's no doubt that we have a huge unmet need in terms of the options available to such people.

The most popular tools used in the treatment of these disorders are called selective serotonin reuptake inhibitors (SSRIs).

Selective Serotonin Reuptake Inhibitors (SSRIs)

These are antidepressants that work by increasing levels of serotonin within the brain. We've discussed serotonin briefly in the third chapter. It is a neurotransmitter which is also known as the "feel-good hormone." Though its exact mode of working is still not understood properly, it is widely believed that higher levels of serotonin lead to increased well-being, better mood, and better appetite. Not only that, but it also helps in regulating the sleep cycle of our bodies, a cycle that has an effect on our mood in the long term. It is believed that, when there is more serotonin available in the nerve synapse, it is easier for it to transmit messages. The easier it is to transmit these messages, the healthier the brain is. Since it is believed that depression is caused due to lower levels of serotonin in the brain, it makes sense that antidepressants work by enhancing the serotonin levels. Also, they are used to treat anxiety, PTSD, addiction, and other disorders.

SSRIs are the most common type of antidepressants, though there are a few others. These include tricyclic antidepressants (TCAs), serotonin and norepinephrine reuptake inhibitors (SNRIs), norepinephrine and dopamine reuptake inhibitors (NDRIs), monoamine oxidase inhibitors (MAOIs), and the atypical antidepressants.

Some FDA-approved SSRIs (along with their brand names) to treat depression are:

- Citalopram (Celexa)
- Fluoxetine (Prozac)
- Sertraline (Zoloft)
- Escitalopram (Lexapro)
- Paroxetine (Paxil, Pexeva)

Concerns Around SSRIs

Though it is generally said that SSRIs are safe, with relatively few side effects, there are quite a few concerns around their usage. Some of the common side effects are:

- dry mouth
- insomnia
- nervousness, agitation, or restlessness
- dizziness
- drowsiness
- headaches
- nausea, vomiting, and diarrhea
- impact on appetite and weight

Apart from these side effects, there are real safety issues with most SSRIs. For example, high doses of citalopram may cause abnormal heart rhythms that might be dangerous. The FDA recommends taking less than 40 mg each day, whereas adults over the age of 60 should not take more than 20 mg per day.

Another concern faced by most people is related to drug interactions. Most SSRIs interact with certain medications in a dangerous manner, or they reduce the effectiveness of said medications. Therefore, you should clearly disclose to your doctor any information regarding existing medication, be it herbal or over-the-counter pharmaceuticals. For example, if you take nonsteroidal anti-inflammatory drugs

(NSAIDs), aspirin, warfarin (Coumadin, Jantoven), and other blood thinners, you might be at an increased risk of bleeding due to SSRIs.

Serotonin syndrome is a rare condition that occurs when there are high levels of serotonin in the brain. It occurs mostly when two separate medications are being taken, each known to increase serotonin levels in the brain. These medications could include other antidepressants, certain pain and headache medicines, and the herbal supplement St. John's wort. It is a dangerous condition and requires immediate medical attention. Symptoms to look out for include anxiety, agitation, high fever, sweating, confusion, tremors, restlessness, lack of coordination, major changes in blood pressure and a rapid heart rate.

If a woman is pregnant or is considering getting pregnant, she needs to talk to her doctor about the possible risks to themselves and their baby, as some can cause serious harm to the infant during pregnancy or breast-feeding.

The FDA requires that all antidepressants carry black-box warnings, which are the strictest warnings for prescriptions. This is because, in some cases, teenagers or young adults under the age of 25 have reported an increase in suicidal thoughts or behavior, especially during the first few weeks of taking these antidepressants or when there is a change in dose. In general, it is advised to be cognizant of changing moods or worsening depression while taking antidepressants and to talk to your doctor immediately if something is wrong.

While SSRIs aren't considered addictive, abrupt discontinuation of the treatment or missing out on too many doses can lead to withdrawal-like symptoms, including uneasiness, nausea, flu-like symptoms, dizziness, and lethargy. This phenomenon is known as the "discontinuation syndrome," and therefore it is necessary to work with your doctor while decreasing doses or changing medication.

Adapting to SSRIs is also a valid concern for most people. Many people have trouble adjusting to some SSRIs, while others might find that what works for some people does not work for them. So, it is a question of efficacy as well. It is suggested that, if a close relative takes antidepressants which work for them, there is a good chance that these might work for the concerned person as well. This implies that genetics have an important role to play in the efficacy of these drugs.

These are concerns around safety and side effects, but what about results? After all, for decades, these SSRIs have been the only available options to people struggling with various mental health disorders.

Questions Around Efficacy

According to the American Journal of Psychiatry, almost one in eight people in the US were on antidepressants throughout the nation. This number, likely, could only have gone up with the Covid-19 pandemic and the resulting mental health pandemic. Unfortunately, more than a third of these patients had become resistant to the mood-enhancing benefits of these antidepressants. This raises important questions as to whether the effects of these drugs aren't largely placebo effects which fade over time.

The second issue with SSRIs is that they usually take several weeks to show any real effects. In fact, it is expected that the first few weeks or longer will be full of adjustments and side effects rather than any benefits in curing the symptoms of depression. Related to this is the question of how long the effects last because it is seen that people need to stay on antidepressants for a long time in order for the effects to be somewhat long-term. Even then, there is no guarantee that reducing the dose or going off medication will ever be an option.

It is clear that SSRIs cannot be the only options available to people and that there is a need for something better. The question is: Are psychedelics capable of filling this gap, and if so, how?

A Ray of Hope

Let us now talk about psychedelic-assisted psychotherapy and how it could become transformative in the outlook of the mental health profession.

Safety

First and foremost, psychedelics are remarkably safe to use. This is a nuanced discussion, however, and not an invitation to use them for recreational purposes blatantly. There are two things that should be of utmost consideration. One is the correct dose and the other is the combination of set and setting. This is also why many therapists repeatedly stress the reasoning behind why this method is called psychedelic-assisted psychotherapy. When you take the substances under clinical conditions as part of trials conducted at reputable institutions, the dose will be securely monitored. At the same time, you will be properly screened, checked for any previous conditions that might cause issues (psychosis is one of them), and prepared thoroughly for the treatment. This preparation may sometimes take hours and with good reason. It is essential that the patient set the intention for their treatment themselves. They should know what they are expecting from the treatment, which makes it difficult for a truly blind study to occur but increases the efficacy of the drug. They should also not have any previous anxiety or fear because that is what increases the chances of having a challenging journey or feeling nauseated. They might experience hallucinations, but the chances are greatly reduced when they are told that the treatment will be relaxing. The patients should also be able to trust their guides and know that they are available in case of any need. All of this takes time and skill, which is why these medicines should be taken in safe and supportive environments to see their results. When most of these conditions are set in place, there are almost no issues concerning lack of safety.

Efficacy

When it comes to efficacy, there are two aspects to consider. Firstly, most of the trials that have been successfully conducted around psychedelics have only administered a single dose of the substances over a single session. As we shall soon see in the studies discussed further in the chapter, they have been remarkably effective in treating the disorders through a single dose. In fact, the trials that were underway in the Usona Institute used a single dose of psilocybin to treat its patients for major depressive disorder (MDD).

Usona Institute is one of many organizations that is working towards improving mental health of people through psychedelics. Based in Madison, Wisconsin, Usona is a 501(c)(3) non-profit medical research organization dedicated to supporting and conducting pre-clinical and clinical research to further the understanding of the therapeutic effects of psilocybin and other consciousness-expanding medicines. It was founded in 2014 by Bill Linton, CEO and Founder of the international life sciences company Promega Corporation, and Malynn Utzinger, M.D., Director of Integrative Practices at Promega Corporation. Linton was inspired to open the institute after he witnessed the impact that the psilocybin study at Johns Hopkins had on his friend, who was suffering from the debilitating effects of terminal cancer. Its stated mission is to alleviate depression and anxiety in patients who haven't been granted relief by the current medications available to them. It is supported by various research organizations and scientists, including Griffiths, Grob, and Carhart-Harris.

The second aspect of efficacy relates to the long-term effects of the substances. In many cases, the effects last way beyond the session and, in some cases, are permanent. In general, psychedelics have a longer-lasting effect as compared to an SSRI regimen. In 2015, Johns Hopkins conducted a nationwide survey of more than 190,000 Americans with a past history of psychedelic use. The results indicated that past history of psychedelic use (mind you, this wasn't even in a controlled setting) decreases the incidence of suicidal thoughts and actions over the years, while other drugs like sedatives and inhalants might actually increase it.

Other Benefits

A 2020 study published in the research journal *PLOS ONE* demonstrates that MDMA-assisted psychotherapy is cost-effective in the treatment of PTSD. Getting better treatment at lower costs surely sounds like a deal we can all get behind, right?

The other benefit, and this might be, by far, the most significant one, is that, while most SSRIs reduce the symptoms of depression and other disorders, psychedelic-assisted psychotherapy might be effective in exterminating the root cause of these disorders. That is a radical idea, but one that is slowly gaining traction in the scientific community. Let us discuss some landmark studies that have made all of this possible and what these indicate for the workings of psychedelics in psychotherapy as well as for the future of this exciting field.

Evidence of Psychedelic-Assisted Psychotherapy

In this section, we shall look at a few studies that have used psilocybin to treat addiction as well as depression in patients. The next chapter will discuss the trials held to alleviate existential distress in patients suffering from terminal cancer.

Hope for Those Beyond Hope

Before we look at the various promising studies that are being conducted in this field, let us examine a certain section of people who might benefit immensely from psychedelic-assisted psychotherapy. This group consists of a growing number of soldiers who suffer from PTSD and are turning to psilocybin, LSD, and other psychedelics to treat themselves. It is estimated that about 17% of people who have been a part of active military service report debilitating symptoms such as nightmares, anxiety, depression, flashbacks, anger, and grief. These are all part of their response to the immense trauma they have faced during service. Many of these people suffer for years without any help in sight. In fact, many of these symptoms are so extreme that the veterans cannot experience healing through the widely approved treatment practices. The question is, is there any hope for them?

In 2020, a team at the Medical University of South Carolina reported on clinical trials which proved that psilocybin-assisted psychotherapy for PTSD patients was much more effective than talk therapy or other psychotherapeutic techniques alone. In fact, a new body called the Medical Psychedelic Working Group, which consists of academics, researchers, policy makers, and experts, aims to lobby for changes in the law so that it is easier for scientists to conduct trials with veterans.

Professor David Nutt, who is a part of an independent scientific body that espouses an evidence-based approach to the legislation around psychedelics, says that three years ago he would have believed that veterans shouldn't relive their trauma while on psychedelics. As it turns out, today he is convinced that this scenario works for many veterans.

One such example is that of Guy Murray, an infantryman with the 4th Battalion, The Rifles of the UK. He served a long tour in Afghanistan, where he witnessed the death of his best friend and many colleagues at the hands of Taliban. These horrors reverberated through his mind even after he returned, and he was diagnosed with PTSD in 2017. The official diagnosis came after having suffered from suicidal thoughts, anxiety, and severe depression for many years.

After having gone through other therapeutic methods, he watched a Ted Talk about psilocybin and depression. Curious (and desperate) to see if it worked, he ingested psilocybin, and later LSD, under specialist supervision.

The results were tremendously positive. According to him, those sessions allowed him to address memories and grief that he was usually avoiding at all costs. Confronting his pain allowed him to open up. He stopped being destructive and believes that he cured his PTSD during those sessions.

What's more, experts are of the opinion that Murray's experiences are common among the armed forces.

Not just war veterans, but former pro athletes are also using psychedelics to heal from the trauma and depression caused by their brain injuries. An episode of *Real Sports With Bryant Gumbel* on HBO shows former National Hockey league (NHL) player Daniel Carcillo planning to kill himself. What was the reason behind considering such an extreme step? He was one of many athletes who had been physically, as well as mentally, traumatized by the long-term effects of repeated concussions.

Chronic traumatic encephalopathy (CTE) is a condition of the brain that results due to repeated blows on the head. Some of its major symptoms include memory loss, personality changes, erratic behavior, confusion, headaches and pressure, and depression. Studies show that many of the players of full-contact sports suffer from this condition, which often goes undiagnosed.

For someone like Carcillo, who had suffered from at least seven, and maybe even more, concussions throughout his 12-year hockey career, the entire experience left him feeling dead inside. He tried psychotherapy and different SSRIs throughout the years, to no avail. That was when he decided to try psychedelics for the first time.

This experience left him with little-to-no depression and anxiety, and it also eliminated symptoms like slurred speech, memory issues, and insomnia. According to his wife, she saw her husband finally smile after years of somber and pained emotions. What's more, the fact that he had remained symptom-free for months after the sessions makes her vouch for the efficacy of these compounds.

For some people, the cost of following their passions or protecting their country is too high. They end up losing a lot because of their dedicated service and find little-to-no help in alleviating their pain. Psychedelic-assisted psychotherapy gives them hope in the darkness. It is becoming clear to people that these compounds facilitate immense healing, and they need to be given a fair chance by the research community and the policy makers.

Treatment of Addiction Disorders

A pilot study was conducted by Roland Griffiths in his laboratory at Johns Hopkins to study the potential of psilocybin in treating smoking addiction. Smoking addiction is one of the most insidious of afflictions, and people find it notoriously hard to kick this habit. The sample consisted of 15 smokers who had tried to quit multiple times in the past. It was clear that nothing had worked, not even what is considered the most effective therapy to-date: the nicotine patch. It was an open-label study, meaning that there was no placebo control, and the participants knew they were being administered psilocybin.

The results of the study were published in 2014 in the *Journal of Psychopharmacology*. While the sample size was small, the results were nothing short of remarkable. 12 out of the 15 smokers were verified as abstinent six months after the treatment. This is a success rate of 80%. Compare this result to the success rate of nicotine-replacement therapy. In a 2014 article in the *British Medical Journal (BMJ)*, it was reported that the subjects remained abstinent in less than 7% of the cases. Again, this is a small sample, and there is definitely a need to replicate the study on a larger scale, but the difference is far too striking to go unnoticed.

The study required subjects to undergo two or three psilocybin sessions along with CBT to help them deal with cravings. Since the results were brilliant, a larger, second-phase trial was commissioned at Johns Hopkins.

Another treatment for addiction was conducted by MP Bogenschutz and his team, and the results were published in the *Journal of Psychopharmacology* in 2015. This time it focused on alcohol addiction. In this treatment, ten subjects with DSM-IV alcohol dependence (as characterized by the Diagnostic and Statistical Manual of Mental Disorders) were administered psilocybin in one or two supervised sessions, coupled with Motivational Enhancement Therapy (MET). This study included a placebo control. It is noteworthy that the MET alone had not been able to keep them abstinent in the first four weeks of treatment (when psilocybin had not been administered). After psilocybin was administered, abstinence was seen in as little as four weeks. What's more, these gains were largely maintained during a 36-week follow-up. There were no adverse effects reported, and this made it possible for a larger trial to be conducted at New York University.

Treatment of OCD

In 2006, a study was published in the *Journal of Clinical Psychiatry* that sought to understand the effects of psilocybin in OCD treatment. In this open-label study, nine subjects suffering from OCD were administered psilocybin. They were looking to assess not just the efficacy, but also the safety of giving psilocybin-assisted treatment to these patients.

The results indicated that psilocybin was not only safe to administer but was also associated with acute reductions in core OCD symptoms in several subjects. The results were promising enough to warrant a larger study with better design at Yale University.

Treatment of Depression

When the second phase of the trials on terminally ill cancer patients was concluded in 2016, Griffiths brought the results to the FDA in hopes of winning approval for a larger, phase-III trial. What happened was unexpected. While the FDA did not officially confirm or deny this incident, it is reported that the FDA saw potential to treat patients who were not terminally ill but were suffering from depression. This was similar to when, in 2016, the European Medicines Agency (EMA) asked researchers to shift their focus from "existential distress" to general depression. Of course, one reason for this direction was that "existential distress" is not an official DSM diagnosis, so it couldn't be covered by national health services. But the more important reason for the revised focus was that the EMA had been noticing promising studies being conducted not only at Hopkins and NYU, but also at Imperial College. This was the same team that had been working on understanding the neuroscience behind "ego dissolution" as experienced by those under the influence of psilocybin.

This study was published in *Lancet Psychiatry* in 2016 and included six men and six women being treated for treatment-resistant depression. As mentioned earlier, this means that they had already tried two treatments without success. This was also an open-label study, so everyone was aware that they were getting psilocybin-assisted treatment.

While the study was small and not randomized, the results were impressive enough for the EMA to suggest a larger trial for treatment-resistant depression. Within a week, each of the twelve volunteers showed improvements in their symptoms, while two-thirds of them reported being depression-free, some of them for the first time in years. After three months, seven of the twelve volunteers showed that those benefits persisted.

Later, the study was expanded to include twenty volunteers, out of which six remained in remission after six months. The others had relapsed, suggesting that one dose might not be enough to fully alter their depression, and the treatment might need to be repeated. Even so, the results were highly positive in general, especially keeping in mind that these people were being treated for treatment-resistant depression.

It has become clear that the medical and regulatory bodies are seeing remarkable potential in the use of psilocybin for psychotherapy. There are some interesting aspects of these studies. Firstly, in the smoking addiction treatments, many of the subjects had given up smoking completely. They realized that they didn't need to smoke and stopped. Just like that. Secondly, in the treatment for depression, many subjects reported feeling better after years or maybe for the first time in their lives. Even the remission rates were quite high. There are some questions that arise out of these events.

More Reason to Rejoice?

Scientists that study addiction know one thing: The patients are fully aware of what they are doing to their physical and mental health. For example, no one who smokes is unaware of the fact that smoking is injurious to health, that they are damaging their lungs, or that they are at an increased risk of cancer. They also know that passive smoking causes harm to those around them, and they are essentially putting their lives at risk as well. It is the same for alcohol addiction. Not only do alcoholics harm themselves physically and mentally, but they also cause immense distress to their family members. In a way, everything assumes less importance than their craving for a drink. Therefore, when we look at treatment for these disorders, the usual treatment includes CBT as well. The major challenge is: How do you convince the subjects of that which they know already? Related to this: How can you effect change when there is no real change in the thought patterns? After all, it isn't like the subjects suddenly wake up to the full impact of their actions. They've known, all along, of the destructive nature of their addictions but aren't able to do anything to modify their impulsive behaviors.

What is it, then, that compels them in the case of psilocybin-assisted psychotherapy? What is this new insight they gain that smoking or drinking becomes unnecessary and irrelevant in their lives?

To understand this, one must examine the experiences as observed by the subjects themselves. Of course, these experiences are completely subjective, but the results are there for everyone to see. Many of the subjects who can maintain their abstinence for a long time say that, when they were under the influence of psilocybin, they could successfully face themselves and their demons. Here, the demons imply tobacco or alcohol. We've already discussed in the third chapter that decreased activity in the DMN causes many regions of the brain to start talking to each other as well as an overabundance of sensory cues. In this scenario, it means that people can actually see their addiction either in the form of thick smoke or in the form of the disfigurement it was causing them. You might ask, so what? What if I'm being shown images or other sensory cues that show how dangerous my addiction really is? This is what brings us to the most important fact about mystical experiences, which is that they make your experience seem objective and true. So, you are not seeing a subjective version of reality like you might in your dreams. Rather, you can see everything as real, perhaps for the first time in your life. This makes it difficult for you to shake off the experience and carry on with your life unaffected. Therefore, it is no coincidence that, the greater the mystical experience reported by the subject, the higher were their chances of staying abstinent for longer.

In the case of depression, it has been mentioned earlier that increased activity in the default mode network (DMN) might be responsible for it. This is true even for addictions and other disorders. The current consensus for most neuroscientists in this field is that many of these disorders are connected to the same part of the brain and similar activity as well. These disorders all fall on the highly ordered end of the spectrum, and therefore, they lead to excessive rumination, increased selfishness (as can be seen in addiction disorders), repetitive harmful behavior, and a greater sense of disconnection from the environment. This is most clearly seen in depression, where even though participants rationally are aware of the state they are in, they are not able to connect to the root causes and to the people that matter to them. Since the DMN is known as the "me network," it makes sense that a stronger ego makes it more difficult to establish meaningful connections with the world outside us.

Why do these discussions matter? For two main reasons. Firstly, it gives us a probable answer to why all these disorders can be effectively treated by one drug or class of drugs. (I prefer to call psychedelics, or more specifically, psilocybin, a medicine; however, medicine and drug is used interchangeably in this text). If all of them arise in the same region or due to the same mechanism of the brain, then it makes sense that treating one will help in treating all of them. In fact, medical professionals have started stressing the idea that these disorders might not be as disparate as they are made out to be and might influence one another much more than initially ascertained. This is also why psychedelic-assisted psychotherapy gives us hope that we might be able to cure the causes and not just the symptoms of these diseases.

Secondly, all these studies and their results keep coming back to one key factor: transcendence. What is transcendence, and why does it hold the key to psychotherapy? Let us find out in the next chapter.

Chapter 6:

Transcendence

Ah, transcendence! In this chapter, we are dealing with a topic that, by its very nature, cannot be contained in words. What do we mean by transcendence? Simply put, it is the state of surpassing our normal life or existence. This sounds inadequate as a definition, and it is, because the kind of transcendence that people witness on psilocybin defies imagination and concrete definition. It is also impossible to witness someone else's ego-dissolution, not least because we might not be able to take it.

The question that we have to answer is this: Why bother with a state of being which can neither be adequately described nor properly understood? We have been dealing with different instances of transcendence throughout this book, and one can argue that transcendent experiences were what led to so many psychonauts to forge new paths in psychedelics. These experiences have been transformative, but how are they useful as a discussion on psychotherapy?

The Mystical Experience

What constitutes a mystical experience? No one knows the exact answer to that, but some philosophers and religious thinkers have attempted to answer it. There are three convictions that have arisen from various experiments using psychedelics in the past. One is that the experiences of the sacred as reported by mystics and those reported by high-dose psychedelics are real and of related experiential instances. This was also supposed to be proven in the Good Friday Experiment conducted on the divinity students. The second conviction is that these experiences form the primary basis of religion. That is, a religion is formed when someone has a divine experience or witnesses a true miracle and then wants to impart the wisdom to others. The third one, which is probably the most controversial one, is that consciousness is a property of the universe rather than the brain. Remember how Terence McKenna thought that consciousness arose as a result of eating psychoactive mushrooms? In the same way, many mystics believe that consciousness doesn't belong to the brain in the first place, which causes a lot of problems for those trying to understand it, but more on that later.

Philosopher and historian William James in his book *The Varieties of Religious Experience* describes the four qualities of a mystical experience. These qualities are:

a) Ineffability—The inability to capture or describe the experience in ordinary language.
b) Noetic quality—The idea that these experiences reveal an otherwise hidden or inaccessible knowledge.
c) Transiency—The fact that these experiences last for a relatively short period of time.
d) Passivity—The sense that these experiences happen to us, and we have no say or control over them.

While these are the four official qualities, there are others that are connected to mystical experience. For example, transcendence is a quality of a mystical experience. You seem to transcend time, space, and the very concept of "I." This transcendence is also what leads to a feeling of unity or oneness with the universe. You are indistinguishable from the universe. The concept of "ego dissolution" is central to the experience of transcendence.

Remember the mushroom rituals in the ancient cultures, most notably the Maya and Aztec cultures? These rituals had nothing to do with therapy and everything to do with communion with the Divine. How can transcendence help in psychotherapy, or the quality of life in general?

Transcendence and Psychotherapy

Let us revise what we learned in the previous chapter regarding psilocybin in psychotherapy. When we discovered the miraculous effects that psilocybin had on patients with mental disorders, we also realized that a major reason behind their success was attributed to this feeling of transcendence, as reported by the subjects. In the case of addiction, those who reported having intense mystical experiences were able to abstain from their affliction for a longer period. What did these mystical experiences tell them? Quite simply, it told them that they no longer existed, and that they were one with the universe. They saw and felt things that were beyond their scope of imagination. The effect this had on them was to tell them that smoking, or alcohol consumption was inconsequential in the grand scheme of things. This feeling made it easier for them to kick their habit for good. So convinced were they of their visions that they didn't even crave what they had given up.

What happened in the case of depression? The subjects reported feeling a sense of connectedness to the universe as they had never felt before. In some cases, they went from simply enjoying nature to feeling one with it. This feeling of oneness, as we know, is another hallmark of the mystical experience.

What do these mean in terms of neuroscience? As we have studied earlier, these experiences disrupt our normal waking consciousness; as Carhart-Harris says, they "shake the snow globe." They tell us that there are different states of consciousness available for us to experience. In fact, many researchers are beginning to question that, if what we think of as reality is but another state of consciousness, then what makes this reality any more real than another? A scary thought, but also an interesting one.

Before we discuss the effects of transcendence and mystical experiences in psychotherapy, let us learn a little bit about the exciting research that is being conducted in this field. The first major controlled study done on mystical experiences was the Good Friday Experiment that was discussed in the second chapter. A follow-up by Rick Goblin had confirmed that these experiences had a profound effect on the students, even after many years, though he had raised doubts regarding the quality of the study.

Remember Bob Jesse and the Council on Spiritual Practices? In their 1996 meeting, they had decided to conduct high-quality research on psilocybin and possibly other psychedelics with the sole aim of exploring their spiritual potential. In 2006, Jesse along with Bill Richards and Roland Griffiths conducted an experiment loosely based on the Good Friday Experiment and tried to measure not only the psychotherapeutic, but the transcendental nature of the experience. It was a double-blind study where all 36 participants were hallucinogen-naive adults. They reported regular activity in religious or spiritual activities. Thirty of the volunteers received orally administered psilocybin and a placebo named methylphenidate hydrochloride in counterbalanced order. In order to obscure the study design, six additional participants were given methylphenidate in two sessions and unblinded psilocybin in a third session. These sessions were eight hours long and were conducted individually. The participants were encouraged to close their eyes and direct their attention inward. There were study monitors to rate their behavior during sessions. Additionally, they were given questionnaires that assessed the effects of the medicine as well as mystical experiences. These questionnaires were provided immediately after the sessions as well as two months later.

The results were published in a 2006 paper by Roland Griffiths et al. in the *Journal of Psychopharmacology*. It is remarkable that a paper which made no pretense of exploring the psychotherapeutic effects of psilocybin was published in a well-respected journal in the field. The title of the paper was "Psilocybin Can Occasion Mystical-type Experiences Having Substantial and Sustained Personal Meaning and Spiritual Significance."

The results showed that psilocybin led to a range of acute perceptual changes, subjective experiences, and easily altered moods, including anxiety. It also increased measures of mystical experiences. Even more remarkably, volunteers reported that, even after two months, the changes in their behavior and perception remained and had caused lasting effects on their outlook and awareness. This was assessed not only through their own experiences, but also through community assessors.

The participants said that this experience was as meaningful as the birth or the death of a loved one. Such was the spiritual significance of taking psilocybin that they felt forever changed in a positive way.

In 2011, Katherine Maclean conducted a follow-up study with 52 volunteers. This paper was also published in 2011 in the *Journal of Psychopharmacology* entitled "Mystical Experiences Occasioned by the Hallucinogen Psilocybin Lead to Increases in the Personality Domain of Openness." The main aim of this study was to understand if mystical experiences bring about a lasting personality change in adults over the age of 30. It is generally believed that the core personality traits of adults become stable after 30. This study tried to pick up the thread of the previous study which had suggested that mystical experiences can lead to a change in behaviors and attitudes of the subjects.

The subjects were tested on the five domains of personality, namely Neuroticism, Extroversion, Openness, Agreeableness, and Conscientiousness. Following a high-dose session, the participants reported an increase in imagination, creativity, and aesthetic perception. There was also a significant increase in Openness in almost all adults. Even more intriguing was the fact that this trait was exhibited at higher levels even after one year of the session.

These studies were important for various reasons. The most important of the reasons is also perhaps the most ironic. While these studies didn't claim to have anything to do with psychotherapy, they helped influence neuroscience and psychotherapy through a better understanding of transcendence. The major finding that both papers came up with was that mystical experiences could occasion a change, a lasting change no less, in the attitudes and behaviors of otherwise healthy adults. This is a revolutionary idea that can be used to explain addictions and other disorders. After all, the rut that we all find ourselves in after a certain age and accept as our fate might only exist in our imagination. Since these disorders are supposedly a result of repetitive behaviors that cannot be changed, there is renewed hope in altering these behaviors for good. Remember how the smokers had tried multiple times to quit? The incredible way in which they could change such a stubborn habit after a few sessions of psilocybin administration can now be explained.

There is something even better to consider in light of these results. Neuroplasticity is the condition that allows us to change our modes of thinking and behaving. Meditation is thought to influence neuroplasticity, and so are experiences of awe. What about psilocybin? As it turns out, the ability to make our moods and minds more flexible indicates that even temporary neuroplasticity might help us change our behaviors for good.

Transcendence as a Cure for Existential Distress

Perhaps the greatest influence that the concept of transcendence has had on psychotherapy is in easing the existential angst of terminally ill cancer patients. What is existential distress? It is defined as the psychological turmoil experienced by individuals when faced by imminent death. This turmoil affects them physically, mentally, emotionally, and not least of all, spiritually. They find themselves, as well as their relationships, tested during this time.

To know that you will cease to exist as "you" in a matter of months or even years is an unnerving experience. This is a time when even the otherwise devout people experience a crisis of faith. How, if at all, can psilocybin or any psychedelic help ease their pain during this time?

It should be noted that using psychedelics to treat existential distress in terminally ill patients is not a new phenomenon. In fact, Aldous Huxley had used it just before his death, and Sidney Cohen was involved in many such studies as well. While the results were optimistic, the studies themselves were poorly designed. It was in 2010 that Charles Grob led a trial at Johns Hopkins and enrolled 12 adults with advanced-stage cancer and anxiety. The aim was to be able to ease the anxiety experienced by these subjects' using psilocybin. It was a placebo-controlled design and administered a moderate dose of psilocybin to all the subjects. Follow-up data included results from the Beck Depression Inventory, Profile of Mood States, and State-Trait Anxiety Inventory. This data was collected unblinded for six months after treatment. There were no adverse effects reported due to the administration. The results were published in 2011 in *JAMA Psychiatry* and reported a significant decrease in anxiety at one and three months after the treatment. Depression also reduced significantly, and the effects were maintained at six months as well. The participants reported feeling calmer about their fate and having come to terms with their impending death. This was not all; they felt more connected to the world and believed that they had seen things that they couldn't have imagined. The experiences were varied. Some "saw" their death. Some saw how they became manure for trees to grow after their death. Some understood that whatever they had witnessed as life was an illusion, and they understood what life, and death, was all about. These experiences made them feel better about the last few months or years left in their lives. They also felt more connected to their loved ones and became grateful for their presence. They cherished each moment with them and prepared them for what was to come.

While the sample size was small, the results were astounding. So much so that the *New York Times* ran a cover story in the same year entitled "Hallucinogens Have Doctors Tuning In Again." This was the first time that a well-controlled study had been conducted, and it left researchers all over the US hopeful that this could be a promising new beginning in the field of end-of-life care.

In December 2016, Griffiths conducted a larger study comprising 51 advanced-stage cancer patients with anxiety and depression. A very low dose of psilocybin (acting as a placebo) was administered versus a high dose of psilocybin in a counterbalanced sequence. The sessions had a break of five weeks in between, and there was a six-month follow-up as well. Throughout the study, participants, staff, and community observers rated the moods, attitudes, and behaviors of the participants.

The results showed that psilocybin produced significant decreases in both self- and clinician-rated measures of anxiety and depression. Not only that, but the resulting data also indicated an increase in quality of life, optimism, and meaning of life as well. The six-month follow-up showed that these effects were sustained for 80% of the participants. Similar studies were conducted across other institutions after seeing the promising results of these trials. These trials also gave policy makers and regulatory bodies the confidence to conduct even larger trials related to depression.

That these trials influenced the course of history is obvious. What is more intriguing is that psilocybin was able to achieve something that is objectively difficult to achieve. Not only did it lead to reduced instances of anxiety and depression in these patients, but also led to an improvement in quality of life. The kind of depression that people facing imminent death go through is marked by a lot of angst. The usual question is, "Why me?" "What did I do to deserve this?" and so on. In one way, the ego becomes prominent again because death seems like a final thing, which means that the subjective "I" is in danger. At the same time, the patient is so focused on the dying aspect that they cannot feel connected to those they love. Life itself seems meaningless and without purpose.

It is here that psychotherapy using psychedelics seems to bridge the gap between mystical experiences and neuroscience. While we may still be unable to answer whether depression and other disorders are a result of a purely chemical imbalance or if it is a loss of meaning and purpose that makes us feel this way, one thing is clear: Mystical experiences imbue our lives with meaning and purpose, and at the same time fill us with awe (which supposedly has an effect on the DMN). We feel connected with everything here and beyond, and our consciousness expands beyond what we deemed possible before.

Most importantly, the "I" that we are so desperately hanging onto seems to dissolve, and we realize that this "I" does not exist. Once that vanishes, what is left to lament?

I cannot pretend that a topic as vast and complex as transcendence can be dealt with within the space of a chapter, or indeed a book. What gives me hope is that recent events have made conversations around this topic possible and accessible. Whenever humans decide to accept that there might exist realities beyond their own, it benefits humanity as a whole.

Finding Hope in the Darkest Places

The next story is of someone who has stared into the existential abyss for years on end. Every moment they lived reminded them of their mortality. Having given up on finding peace with themselves, they found themselves getting a second lease of life.

This is the story of Dr. Lauren Macdonald, a psychiatrist and integrative medicine specialist. Her story begins at what could have been the end. In February 2014, she was diagnosed with malignant melanoma, the deadliest form of skin cancer known to us. She underwent multiple surgeries and treatments, but after a year and a half of treatments, the cancer had progressed to stage IV, which led to the rapid growth and spread of tumors in her lymph nodes, pectoral muscles, and lung and adrenal glands. She was 31 years old, with a prognosis of about a year left in her life.

This led to insomnia and anxiety, which manifested in late-night Google searches for anti-cancer foods and supplements, stories of stage IV melanoma survivors, and anything that would bring her hope. It also led to a deep existential dread unlike anything she had ever known. The irony was that, as a doctor, she was trained to diagnose anxiety and depression in people. However, nothing could have prepared her for the overwhelming hopelessness and dissociation that one feels because of being diagnosed with a terminal illness.

What happened in the next year or so was nothing short of a miracle. Lauren was able to get access to a cutting-edge new treatment through the National Health Service (NHS). This was at the beginning of 2016, when she underwent immunotherapy, and after six months, her scans showed No Evidence of Disease (NED). She has been given a second chance at life, after having lost hope completely. However, this miracle was only the first one. She was yet to experience a miracle that would bring hope back into her life.

You see, even though she had miraculously been cured, she was left with a lingering fear of recurrence and death. She could feel the fragility of life weighing down on her, and as we all know, that is no way to live life. In 2018, while she was still dealing with the physical and psychological scars left behind by the cancer, she was hit by a vehicle as a pedestrian. As a result, she was left wheelchair-bound for many months. This triggered her anxiety even further, and she found herself in constant "flight-or-fight" mode.

It wasn't that she didn't try to mitigate her anxieties. Meditation, yoga, journaling, talk therapy, breathwork, even cold-water swimming, were all undertaken, and she tried each of them in hopes of feeling better. However, she knew that she was still living only a half-life, if that. After having tried everything she could, she came across the possibility of using psilocybin to deal with her issues.

Like others, she was wary of psychedelics. She had heard of bad trips and events resembling psychosis in people and didn't want to take any risks, especially when she was feeling so fragile. However, when she came across the trial conducted at Johns Hopkins to reduce end-of-life distress in terminal cancer patients in 2016, she felt hopeful and somewhat reassured. What gave her even more confidence was a TED talk by Roland Griffiths. Finally, in October 2019, she travelled to a retreat in the Netherlands, hoping that psilocybin-assisted psychotherapy might be the answer to years of trauma faced due to both the cancer as well as the accident.

The first few days at the retreat were dedicated to getting the "set" and "setting" right. To do this, all participants were encouraged to sing, dance, meditate, spend time in the garden, sit in sharing circles, and listen to fireside stories. This led to Lauren feeling more relaxed and less self-conscious each day. She also began to feel more present in her body.

On the day of the ceremony, she sang beautiful folk songs with the group as they crushed the truffles to put in their tea. Before drinking the mushroom-infused tea, they added their personal items to an altar and set their intentions for the journey ahead. In this way, they were in the proper state of mind to begin.

Lauren lay down, covered her eyes, and pulled the blanket up to her chin. All at once, she started seeing geometric shapes and colors. They were breathtakingly beautiful and nothing like anything she had seen before. The music that was playing in the background (or her mind) directed the geometric patterns that were dancing in front of her eyelids. They affected both the quality and intensity of her emotions. Consequently, she lost track of time and soon experienced a state of ego-dissolution. No "me" existed for her, and everything became pure energy. She felt the presence of people from her past, but not as humans. Instead, they were all beautiful swirling energy forms that told her that death is not final, but simply an end to our physical form. This insight brought her peace.

Then, she heard the "quiet sound of mournful crying" in the distance. She felt the presence of a facilitator trying to comfort her and realized that she was the one who was crying. Feeling safe and supported allowed her to release years of pain. The music shifted as years of sadness slowly dissipated. As she placed her hands on her chest and belly and took a deep breath, the music became a tribal drumming, along with a lady singing in an unrecognizable language. This music placed her inside her own body, where she found her ancestors in the form of wolves, waiting to guide her through the next part of her journey.

After her experience at the retreat, both Lauren's life as well as her perception of psilocybin was changed forever. She went in hoping that she would rid herself of at least some of the fear and anxiety around her mortality but returned with a lot more than she had anticipated. In her own words, it helped her come back to life. She now feels more connected to herself, her friends, family, and, also, the planet, as a whole. She has always had an appreciation of nature, but now she is truly alive to the wonders of the world. She also believes that we are all interconnected, and in helping each other, we are opening ourselves to healing and transformation.

While Lauren emphasizes the importance of getting the right "set," "setting," and "integration" while dealing with psychedelics, her experiences have made her an advocate for their therapeutic use. She believes that they are a potential gateway to "cathartic experiences akin to rebirth."

Changing the Narrative, One Trial at a Time

In the last two chapters, we have seen how psilocybin has shown immense potential for healing many disorders of the mind. It is also known to occasion transcendental experiences, which lead to unparalleled growth for the people concerned. It has been emphasized repeatedly that psychedelics should be administered in clinical settings and in the presence of therapists. The results from these clinical trials have been promising, to say the least. For the first time in a long time, we have hope that diseases of the mind, even those like treatment-resistant depression, can be treated with the help of psychedelics. One might ask, "What about the people who have participated in these trials?" This is the story of a person whose life was changed through one of these trials.

For almost two decades of his life, Steve Shorney worked as a television writer and earned both money and accolades in the process. However, the dark cloud of depression that hovered over his life, over a period of twenty years, made it impossible for him to write. Not only did it suppress his creativity, but it also made it impossible for him to live life fully. He had all but given up on finding a solution, but as it stands, he is now writing again, and has embraced life in a way that he previously thought was impossible. How did this happen? Well, he was one of 60 volunteers who were part of a clinical trial done at Imperial College which was designed to test psilocybin's potential as a treatment for depression.

This trial was led by Robin Carhart-Harris and his team and was funded by many influential personalities, including Tim Ferriss, who believed in the potential of the medicine. Shorney's depression started in his early thirties. His imagination, and his passion for creating stories, became his own worst enemies. He started suffering from catastrophic thoughts that weren't entirely rational. These thoughts included his life, career, and his loved ones. He couldn't sleep properly and found himself tormented by his own mind. For example, when he was making a documentary on the drug trade, he was involved in interviewing convicts who described their worlds with shame and hopelessness. Strangely enough, he also felt the same way, without there being any rational explanation for his thoughts and feelings.

In an effort to numb his pain, he would take refuge in alcohol, which gave him temporary relief, but no real solutions. He knew that he needed to do something when his anger and frustration started disrupting his life and the lives of those around him. Thankfully, he didn't hurt others during his outbursts, but he knew that it was extremely dangerous to continue with this behavior.

When he started looking for solutions from professionals, he first gave cognitive behavioral therapy (CBT) a try. Well-intentioned therapists introduced him to eating and exercise plans and, also, encouraged him to talk about his past experiences. However, he soon realized that he needed to go deeper within himself to understand exactly what the problem was and how to cure it. After realizing that CBT was not working for him as well as it should, he started running, and eventually, got introduced to yoga and meditation. While meditation helped him calm his mind and have more control over his thoughts, yoga helped him get out of his mind and into his body. As a result, he started eating better, and he felt lighter than he had in a long time. However, Shorney was still suffering from frequent bouts of depression.

This is when a psychiatrist suggested to him that the issue might lie in his brain chemistry, and hence, the only solution might be an antidepressant. Even though Shorney had his reservations, he was willing to try anything. Sure enough, the first week on the pill was horrible and disorienting, but after the second week, he was able to adjust to its effects. The biggest challenge for him was that he felt lost, as if an essential part of him was missing. This is an experience that most people on antidepressants have. However, he too, like most others, believed that this was a necessary trade for his peace of mind. Even though he didn't feel whole, he kept taking these antidepressants for almost 10 years. It was around the same time that he started his own yoga and meditation practice, which introduced him to different life-enhancing practices. Still, the question of whether he would ever get truly better persisted. He also wondered why he continued to suffer from depression and what it was that he was missing.

According to Shorney and those therapists who helped him along the way, the issue was that his mind had formed a negative narrative of his life. He was fixated on his bad decisions and wrong choices. Since he was prone to so much rumination, his mind created neural pathways that reinforced these feelings of hopelessness, regret, and guilt. This is why, even though his life had a fair share of ups, in the form of awards as well as close personal relationships, he could not free himself from his self-destructive thought patterns. Therefore, the challenge was to change these negative thinking patterns into positive ways of thinking.

According to the team at Imperial College, this could be achieved through psilocybin-assisted psychotherapy. All 60 volunteers for the trial shared two commonalities — a history of treatment-resistant depression and no previous exposure to psychedelics. The hope was that psilocybin would create enough randomness or disorder in the brain of these people to help them conquer their depression. For Shorney, there was another reason to take part in the trial. He wanted to explore his mind and understand the effects of psilocybin on consciousness. All the big questions that experts were grappling with had also crossed his thoughts for many years. Therefore, he decided to enroll in the trial.

Before he could be a part of the psychedelic experience itself, however, he needed to be a part of the pre-trial screenings. This was essential because he needed to be in a good frame of mind to fully benefit from the experience. Again, this is related to the importance of set and setting during a psychedelic experience. It surprised him that, even in a clinical trial, the environment was friendly, warm, and welcoming, and he realized that this was by design. While he admitted to feeling nervous as well as excited, Shorney was reassured by the presence of two therapists who encouraged him to breathe through the experience and to reach out to them if he needed them at any stage. After this rehearsal, he felt more confident about going through with the actual experience.

The next day, he ingested five white capsules, reclined comfortably on the hospital bed, donned a blindfold and headphones, and waited for the experience to take over. The entire process took about eight hours and was recorded on video.

While he admits that the psychedelic experience, by definition, is ineffable, he has tried to explain how the experience made him feel and why it had such a profound effect on him. By his own admission, he is not a religious person, but the experience was essentially transformative and mystical. In his description of the experience, he says that he was not himself anymore. He was a tree, and then roots, spreading underground and reaching out into infinity, at the same time unbound by place or time, and interconnected with all life. While he knew he was present in the hospital room with two therapists, he also knew that he was present in another dimension, one where he was experiencing life more fully than he had ever before. He came away from the experience having seen an alternative reality, another way of being, and a conviction that life is extraordinary. As a result, he felt happier and more alive than he had in decades.

There was another aspect to the experience that helped him. Not only was he able to see the possibilities that life offered him, but he was also able to confront his inner demons. In the first session, he had to face his fear of death, which seemed like a snake coiled tightly inside him. Recognizing that this fear was not unique to him alone made him feel more capable of dealing with it.

While the first experience was revelatory, the second experience was transformative, in his opinion. They were also very different from each other, highlighting to him that no two psychedelic experiences are the same. During this session, the setting was the same as before, but the set was different. Due to an accident on a motorbike, he found himself sore in body and mind. After his therapists made him feel comfortable and gave him something to ease his physical pain, he settled down for his experience. In the beginning, he felt that there was nothing except darkness. Slowly, in the void, he saw what he felt was something that Adam had seen "on the morning of his creation — the miracle, moment by moment, of naked existence."

He felt himself being carefully picked apart until there was no "me" left. Time lost all meaning, as he felt sensations that reached beyond his dispersed self. Eventually, he found himself overflowing with love. This peak experience was followed by some of the darkest hours in his life. He had to deal with shadows that made him confront his suppressed emotions as well as negative beliefs. While he had never been not willing to explore those sides of himself, confronting them helped him release his demons and feel a sense of gratitude.

As profound as his sessions were, he realized that they were not the destination that he had been seeking. In fact, they were the beginning of a new journey. For him, the greatest effect that psilocybin had on his psyche was that it made him see life differently. With his perspectives challenged and changed for the better, he has been able to embrace life in all its forms. He understood that this effect was permanent when his business ran into trouble due to factors outside his control (Brexit, Covid-19 pandemic, etc.). Earlier, he would have buckled under the pressure, given up, and complained about the unfairness of it all. As it turns out, he has been more than ready to face the challenges life has thrown at him this time around. Not only business, but his personal life has also seen the positive impact of the experience. He is more content than he has ever been, more grateful, and smiles more easily.

Even on an otherwise gray and cloudy day, he can see and appreciate the beauty around him. This is in sharp contrast to earlier times when he would grumble about the weather and refuse to engage with the world on these days.

Shorney feels that the post-trial support offered by the Imperial therapists is just as important a part of the journey. In fact, without proper integration of the psychedelic experience into the real world, most people might end up feeling more confused than excited. He feels this is an exciting time for psychedelics in psychotherapy, and if used responsibly, these compounds can pave the way for a new future in mental health.

Shorney was not the only person who saw his years of depression being cured through psilocybin-assisted psychotherapy. Kirk Rutter was another one of the volunteers who decided to take part in the trial in the hopes of finally putting an end to his depression. This was the year 2015, and Rutter had already spent years battling the disease. It had become much worse after 2011, when he had to deal with the death of his mother, the break-up of a relationship, and a car accident in quick succession. Having had to face what seemed like unrelenting bad times, he felt his brain being stuck on what he calls "an automatic circuit." In other words, he felt responsible for the stroke of bad luck he was having and kept blaming himself for it. Eventually, he had started believing that he was cursed. It had become somewhat of a mantra for him, with all its power for destruction. What's more, years of talk therapy and anti-anxiety medications had failed to improve his condition, which qualified him for the trial.

He remembers thinking that everyone was warm and welcoming. He was also told that an MRI machine would be used to record his brain activity during the trial. Similar to Shorney, he was prepared for his journey beforehand by the therapists. In order to put him at ease, it was explained that he would have a medicine on hand that could neutralize the effect of psilocybin, if need be. Carhart-Harris also practiced a grounding technique with him, which would help him if he felt overwhelmed.

Rutter remembers how he had burst into tears during the pre-trial session, due to the anticipation and the pressure he felt. He already expected to be feeling a lot and having to unpack a lot of his past traumas in the upcoming sessions. The next day, when he began the session, he saw images of Sanskrit text appear in front of him, after which he saw golden bejewelled structures. Then, his mind began the process of confronting his grief. According to him, the sessions were focused, but flexible. He was able to relax after taking the medicine and also engaged in conversation with Carhart-Harris during his session. Rutter was keen on discussing his resentments, which caused him to ponder about the word "relent" and its etymology. He was already looking for a way to let go of his anger and grief, and the therapist was with him every step of the way.

The first session was followed by a second one including a stronger dose, and there was an integration session in the end to make sense of his experiences. According to Rutter, that experience gave him a much-needed opportunity to look at grief differently. He was able to realize that his grief was not helping anyone, least of all him, and that he should let go of it without feeling like he was betraying himself and his loved ones.

Rutter is convinced that those sessions changed his life for the better. In the weeks following the sessions, he would often wonder if his negative self-talk and obsessive patterns of thinking would return. However, he realized that, perhaps for the first time, he was able to experience a sense of control over his feelings and thoughts. This was something he had not experienced earlier.

After a week or so, as he was out shopping with his friends, he suddenly sensed feeling open and optimistic. The feeling was akin to somebody having opened a window in a stuffy room. Five years later, his depression has not returned.

These two stories show us that even treatment-resistant depression has shown promise of being cured using psychedelic-assisted psychotherapy. When we think of the struggles and pain that millions of people experience daily, we can only be thankful for the fact that there is hope for them after all.

Chapter 7:

The Journey

We have discussed so much about the different ways in which psilocybin can help patients struggling with mental health disorders. There are far too many stories of people who have been positively affected by psilocybin, and in this chapter, I present two of these stories to you. But before you read these stories, let us talk about how psilocybin helps people in dealing with trauma.

What is trauma? It is the response to a deeply disturbing or upsetting event that we face either as children or as adults. These events and the resulting feelings make it impossible for us to cope with them and lead to other problems such as anxiety, depression, or PTSD. They also make us feel utterly helpless. Trauma can be caused due to an accident, the passing of a loved one, or different forms of abuse.

Unfortunately, most, if not all of us, experience some form of trauma or another, especially as children. This is not to say that all of us grow up in scary and unprotected environments. It is more likely that we are exposed to much more than we can handle at that age. When we are at an impressionable age, things have a deeper impact on us, and the fears and anxieties that we experience become a part of our innermost selves. For those children that experience abuse in any form, the impact is more profound. This is not to say that adults don't experience trauma. Many people, especially those that live in difficult conditions or work in dangerous environments, experience PTSD as a result of their experiences. While some people are more emotionally resilient than others, trauma is a difficult thing for anyone to deal with.

What does our mind do in such a scenario? Remember that trauma can have the effect of unraveling us. When we experience wounds as children, it becomes even more difficult to heal those wounds on our own. This is when our ego steps up in a protective gesture. Trauma leaves us with a diminished sense of self, especially as children.

The ego then builds protective walls around our "inner child," the one with those wounds, and keeps it away from our daily lives and existence. It doesn't have a choice; it needs to keep us safe and functional.

The problem arises when the trauma resurfaces in our minds and our lives, often unannounced. When we are least prepared, we feel overwhelmed by emotions or act out without knowing where all of it is coming from. In these moments, there is a chance to acknowledge our wounds, but our ego won't let us do so. The "I" is at work again. How do psychedelics help in treating these wounds and recovering from PTSD? Let us find out through some personal stories.

Facing Trauma Through Psilocybin

This is the story of Krystal Penrose, who in her own words "is an intuitive coach, yoga teacher, and heart-centered entrepreneur." She had been involved in healing and "shadow work" for a long time and is a passionate advocate for using psilocybin to deal with unaddressed trauma. Shadow work refers to the practice of dealing with the parts of yourself that might be repressed due to guilt, shame, or fear. When you commit yourself to shadow work, you are willing to take the steps needed to understand the dark sides of yourself that are hidden even to you. Though difficult to put into practice, it can lead to immense healing in the long run.

In this story, Penrose tells us about how she worked with psilocybin to deal with a blockage that she could feel in her stomach. This blockage was not new and in fact had been a part of her stomach for a decade. To her, it felt like a swirling, nervous feeling that manifested in the form of butterflies or digestion issues.

Despite having studied energy and its effects on the body and mind deeply, she chose to ignore the information that her body had been giving her. She knew that persistent digestion problems without any medical cause could mean that it was her body's way of holding on to trauma. It could literally mean that her body was unable to digest certain fears and anxieties that she had experienced as a child. As someone who had visited and worked with many healers throughout her life, she had been repeatedly told that this was a symptom of PTSD. The trauma she had experienced as a child had helped her become a healer, but she had not yet found a way to deal with it in a healthy manner.

Even after she started acknowledging her trauma and began seeking treatment, nothing seemed to really help. Countless therapies, medications, and healing ceremonies could not help her reconcile with her pain and trauma. Nothing seemed to work — including depression therapy, hypnosis, psychotherapy, and even ayahuasca. The most solace she found was through the "inner child" work with Louise Hay, but she couldn't find complete peace.

Even though she had worked with psychedelics for five years before the experience, she could not find a way to deal with PTSD. Nothing seemed to alleviate the trauma, until she took a medicinal dose of psilocybin. It is worthwhile to mention here that this was not a recreational trip but a psychotherapeutic session. Since she had been working with psychedelics for a long time and had experience in guiding journeys, she was able to take the dose herself. It is not advisable to do so without the presence of a trusted guide in a supportive environment.

As for Penrose, this was the experience that unlocked decades of pain and trauma carefully hidden away in her subconscious. When she closed her eyes after ingesting psilocybin, she saw fractal shapes and patterns taking the forms of demons with large teeth. These demons opened their mouths to invite her into a portal of processing. When she started going down the spiral, her ego tried to stop her by reminding her that it was not safe. However, as the psychedelic took over, her ego began to dissolve, leading to lesser and lesser resistance as she allowed her fear to talk. This fear led her to meet the four-year old girl who was hiding under the blanket, feeling unsafe and unloved. There was shouting in the background, and all she wanted was for someone to hold her.

Slowly, as she allowed herself to descend fully into the experience, she felt the fractal shapes dissolve into a pinkish-amber and take on the form of a mother, a Goddess. This was the first time that she felt nurtured and allowed herself to feel her pain fully. As she cried deeply and freely for the first time in ages, she realized that she had been holding on to so much fear without even realizing it.

According to Krystal, this was a transformative experience like she had never experienced before. Psilocybin allowed her to feel her pain without judgment and held space for her as she identified the source of that pain. Though a lot of work needs to be done after identifying and acknowledging the source of our trauma, this first step is crucial to begin the emotional healing process.

By dissolving her ego, psilocybin made it possible for her to face her fears and her trauma.

Guided Psilocybin Journey

Elissa Goodman is one of LA's premiere cleanse experts and holistic nutritionists. Her focus has been on fighting cancer through accessible and easy measures around diet and lifestyle. She had heard of psilocybin well before she finally decided to try it in a therapeutic setting. She had also read Michael Pollan's bestselling book *How To Change Your Mind* in 2018, and it had really resonated with her. Her experiences with cancer, autoimmune diseases, and past unhealed traumas made her wonder if she should also give psilocybin-assisted psychotherapy a try. She consulted with various healers over the years, including her functional doctor, who thought it might be an effective way for her to counter her anxiety. There were many holistic practitioners that told her something curious. They believed that, when she was ready and the time was right, the mushrooms would choose her. She chose to trust the process.

Goodman had participated in many traditional healing practices like energy healing, meditation, breathwork, reiki, and talk therapy for years. None of these methods had, however, provided her with the awakening she needed. That is, until she decided to opt for psilocybin-assisted psychotherapy.

As someone who had always been deeply interested in the subconscious and its workings, she had felt an urge to go deeper within herself and find out the answers to what she was seeking. She felt that inner peace and calm were simply not in her destiny. Then she decided to embark on her first psilocybin journey. This journey she undertook in her own home in comfortable and familiar surroundings and was accompanied on this journey by a guide who was also a life coach and spiritual counselor. More importantly, he was someone she trusted deeply as a friend and guide.

She also stressed the importance of preparation and intention setting before embarking on the journey. The guide worked with her for a full month, which included two weeks of preparation sessions, the day-long journey itself, and then two weeks of integration. This guide absolutely discourages undertaking the journey without this entire process in place.

During the preparation phase, the guide asked her about her intentions and why she wanted to take this journey in the first place. They discussed her past traumas and wounds, her anxiety issues, and what she wanted to take away from the experience. They even had conversations around death. The guide asked her to keep these intentions in mind before and during the journey.

Her guide convinced her that her mental state on the day of journey would also have an impact on the experience she would have. Therefore, it was important for her to be as calm and relaxed as possible. She spent the morning taking a relaxing bath, doing a meditation and yoga session, and journaling. Before consuming the psilocybin, he made her write down her intentions and then blessed the mushroom before they ate it. Afterwards, he suggested that she close her eyes to focus on the journey inward.

It took thirty minutes for the effects to start showing. In the beginning, as she felt like she was losing control, Goodman started feeling terrified. This was because she was not used to losing control in general. Her guide, however, worked her through it lovingly and asked her to relax, trust, and breathe. He told her that the fear was a way for her ego to protect her and that she needed to breathe through it. Slowly, she started feeling calmer and allowed herself to feel everything she was meant to.

Over time, she was overcome with sensation which was both physical and emotional. She felt like she was floating and being guided by a higher energy. She also felt intense vibrations and had to cover herself with a blanket to ease the vibrations. She felt keenly aware of the beauty of everything she was witnessing. Her guide kept reminding her that this was her own journey and that she would experience it herself. They kept repeating the mantra, "Take me where I need to be, show me what I need to see." This helped her in opening up her senses even more to the journey.

She experienced an urge to release the vibrational energy within her through movement. Her guide, however, reminded her of her intentions and urged her to keep focusing inward to receive the most out of the therapy. She also recalls feeling scared multiple times during the journey, at which points her guide reminded her to take deep breaths. She wasn't even conscious that she was holding her breath, and each time she took a deep breath, she felt safer and opened more. It was a way for her fear-based ego to dissolve.

During the journey, Goodman went to some really dark places from her childhood. Though her initial urge was to run away from her demons, she decided to face them, and they led her to experience a kind of self-acceptance and self-love as she had never felt before. Another profound experience on her journey was that she felt the urge to place the huge amount of energy flowing through her on her thyroid and heal it. This was related to her numerous thyroid issues that she had dealt with all her life. She was also able to witness her ego from a distance, and this distance gave her much-needed perspective on how she could self-sabotage frequently and get into trouble. Not only that, but Goodman also confronted another one of her deep-rooted fears - that of losing people who were close to her.

Goodman came away from the experience with some amazing breakthroughs, most of them unexpected. Not only was she able to face her past traumas, but she also saw the pitfalls of her own thinking and behavior. She realized that, in the past, whenever things went awry in her relationships, she was quick to place the blame with the other person. After this experience, she understood where her mistakes lay and how she could become more giving in certain relationships.

Surprisingly, she also realized that she wasn't scared of death anymore, not in the moment anyway. She had this deep feeling that, if she died at that very moment, it would be okay. This was because she realized that she had lived a full life, and the inner peace she had been craving, she had finally received. In fact, she says that the feeling of inner peace persists to this day. After the journey, the guide helped Goodman in describing her experiences as best she could. He also discussed with her some ways in which she could use whatever she had learned on her journey to help live a better and richer life.

After this transformational journey, Goodman has consumed psilocybin multiple times, each time in a safe and supportive environment. According to her, each experience has led to greater insights that have helped her take one more step on her journey to self-discovery. She does issue a caveat, however. She believes that she spent almost 15 years doing a lot of traditional therapy in various forms, and those experiences prepared her for the intensity of this journey. She doesn't like the idea of people jumping in to experience this journey without understanding whether they can handle it, as well as what they need out of it. She has some advice for those who are thinking of undertaking the journey:

- Find a guide who you trust and who is trained in providing therapeutic journeys. The right guide will ensure that your journey is both safe and successful.

- It is highly important to be in the right mental space before taking the journey. This refers to the significance of "set" in psychedelic experiences.
- It is helpful to be prepared. By that, she means that it is a good idea to do some meditation, introspection, or even talk therapy to be prepared for the journey. After all, "ego dissolution" and facing your traumas might be too much for some people.
- "Setting" also plays a very important role in ensuring that your psychedelic journey is the optimum possible one you can experience. This can include having some physical props that can ground you and make you feel calmer. For her, a weighted blanket and eye mask worked wonders.
- The right kind of music might also be helpful for you. Some healers believe that the journey should be completed without any external stimulation, but most think that good music can help evoke certain emotions and thoughts that might otherwise stay hidden.
- After the journey, it is highly important to integrate with your daily life in the proper way. Your guide is essential to this experience, but you should also treat yourself with kindness and empathy once the journey is over. There is a lot that you might not be able to make sense of. At the same time, the feelings from the journey will remain, while the journey will be over, at least for the time being. Make sure you don't rush back into daily life and stay with yourself for some time. You can also journal about your experiences if you feel it will help you, however, resist the urge to overanalyze. The whole experience becomes very impactful if you just "let it be."

In the end, your journey is truly and uniquely yours.

Chapter 8:

The Law: It's Changing

There was a time when psilocybin was legal in the US. It was also at the forefront of psychedelic research. Then came the 1970s and Prohibition. It became a Schedule I drug, which meant that it did not have any potential for medical use and had a high chance of being abused. The bad news first. That status has not yet changed. Psilocybin continues to remain a Schedule I drug under the federal classification. This means that its possession and use carry the highest penalties according to law. Even today, it is difficult to study controlled substances in a clinical setting due to the strict regulations around it.

Decriminalization

In May 2019, Denver, in the state of Colorado, became the first US city to decriminalize psilocybin. It is important to note that decriminalization is not the same as legalization. Psilocybin still remains illegal in Colorado, but the law prevents Denver from spending any resources to prosecute people for the use or possession of psilocybin. This law applies to all adults over the age of 18.

In June 2019, thirty individuals testified to the city council in Oakland, California. These testimonies revolved around their previous experiences with psilocybin. As a result of these testimonies, the council unanimously decided to decriminalize both peyote and psilocybin in the city.

In January 2020, the city of Santa Cruz in California followed suit by voting to decriminalize the adult possession and cultivation of psilocybin, while commercial use of the drug remains illegal.

In September 2020, the city of Ann Arbor, Michigan, voted unanimously to declare the investigation and arrest of anyone for planting, cultivating, purchasing, transporting, distributing, or engaging in practices with or possessing entheogenic plants or plant compounds to be the city's lowest law enforcement priority.

In November 2020, the District of Columbia passed initiative 81, also known as the *Entheogenic Plant and Fungus Act of 2020*, which came into effect on March 15, 2021. This initiative decriminalized psilocybin, making arrests for their use or possession the lowest priority for DC police.

In January 2021, Washtenaw County in Michigan followed suit. In the same month, the City Council of Somerville, Massachusetts, decriminalized entheogenic plants, including psilocybin and ibogaine.

This was followed by Cambridge, Massachusetts, in February 2021; Northampton, Massachusetts, in April 2021; and Seattle, Washington and Arcata, California, in October 2021.

Legalization

In November 2020, Oregon made history by becoming the first US state to legalize psilocybin. Not only that, but it also became the first jurisdiction in the world to lay out plans for regulating the drug's therapeutic use. This is certainly a historic moment and was made possible by many, including therapist Tom Eckert, who co-authored the Oregon Psilocybin Therapy Ballot Measure. This ballot measure was passed by more than 1.2 million votes. According to Tom, the aim of this initiative was to move psilocybin out of the medical framework, to provide safe access to anyone who could benefit from its use.

Needless to say, this move comes with tight regulation measures. Firstly, only licensed therapists and manufacturers will be allowed to grow these psychoactive mushrooms or extract psilocybin from them. This also applies to synthetic production of the drug, setting up psilocybin therapy centers, or providing psilocybin-assisted therapy.

Secondly, only people over the age of 21 can receive the drug, and it can only be consumed at a licensed facility with a certified therapist present. These legal psilocybin centers will also not open until at least 2023, as the measure requires a two-year consultation with lawmakers.

Thirdly, these mushrooms will not be sold at dispensaries for recreational use.

The Future

The people involved with psilocybin-assisted psychotherapy are definitely hopeful. But theirs is a cautious optimism. The ultimate aim is to see psilocybin as a therapeutic medicine available in a regulated market to have more people benefit from it. As for psilocybin retreats, there is a precedent available in the Netherlands, where many of these centers have been opened since 2015 to cater to affluent tourists. Even in the Netherlands, the medicine exists in a legal gray area: psilocybin mushrooms remain illegal, but truffles (clumps of the fungus's subterranean root-like filaments) are termed legal.

The Synthesis Group is a psilocybin retreat center in the Netherlands which is planning to expand into Oregon. According to Rachel Aidan, a professional therapist and CEO of this company, there is a lot to be excited about, but care must be taken. Even Roland Griffiths is of the view that people shouldn't be in a rush to take the medicine out from its tightly regulated settings. Both of them believe that these medicines might not be for everyone in every circumstance and that underestimating the potential side effects might lead to a repeat crackdown of the 1970s, thus undoing a lot of good work that has progressed in this field.

There is much to be hopeful about, as psilocybin is on track to become more mainstream over the next decade or so. As mentioned earlier, you should always keep in mind the laws of the state and not use psilocybin or any psychedelic frivolously.

Conclusion

It feels odd to be concluding a book on psilocybin, knowing that this is but the first page of an exciting new chapter in many of our lives. While psilocybin itself has an ancient history, it has seen many upheavals throughout its time in the public consciousness. This book is an ode to the truly magical mushrooms and their immense potential. Let us do a quick recap before we discuss what the future holds for these entheogens.

The first chapter of the book cast a light on understanding the psychoactive mushrooms through their history as well as the mystique surrounding them. These mushrooms were revered in ancient cultures, and almost none of the great civilizations of the past remained untouched by their influence. There have been some interesting theories around the origin of these mushrooms as well as their impact on us. According to some, we exist as conscious beings because of mushrooms. These mushrooms would have remained largely unknown to the New World if it was not for some pioneers who experienced the effects of these psychoactive compounds and decided to conduct more research into them.

The second chapter took us through the different eras in psychedelic research. The first wave started with the discovery and synthesis of psilocybin and its use in research of various kinds, from spiritual to therapeutic. While most of these studies showed promise in terms of results, they were not controlled or properly designed. Still, a lot was happening during this exciting time, and the government was fully invested in funding research in this area. All that changed with the rise of the counterculture movement in the sixties and seventies, which led to widespread moral panic and paranoia. Even as some psychonauts became vocal advocates of the movement, most chose to withdraw from research in this field because of the stigma around it. This also led to the Prohibition, or the Dark Ages of psychedelics. Many psychonauts still rue the loss of knowledge and opportunities that happened because of the ban on psychedelics. We also learned about the second wave of psychedelic research through its prominent figures and how the studies being conducted during this time are shaping up an exciting future for psychedelics.

The third chapter was all about the neuroscience behind the magic. What is it that makes psilocybin work the way it does? The chemistry of these compounds is relatively easier to understand, but the phenomenology (or the subjective experiences of consciousness) is not. That being said, there are some intrepid researchers that are trying to bridge the gap between the two, and their findings are leading to a new understanding of these compounds and their effects on the brain. While much more needs to be done in this area, it is safe to say that they promise immense potential in psychotherapy. Concepts such as the default mode network and neuroplasticity were discussed along with their implications for the future of neuroscience and psychedelics.

The fourth chapter was all about the pioneers who have ventured boldly forth into new territories. These are the people who have made it possible for research to take on new and improved forms over the years. It is because of them that the "consciousness-expanding" field of psychedelics has seen an expansion. These are the people who haven't given up when the going got tough. They have different personalities as well as different approaches to psychedelic research, but all of them share a passion for these compounds like no other. In this chapter, we have met only five of these psychonauts, but there are many of them that deserve our admiration and respect.

The fifth chapter was centered around healing. The book promises to give you all the details you will need while considering different modes of psychotherapy available to you. This chapter provided a comparison between the well-established, older tools of psychotherapy, namely SSRIs, and psychedelic-associated psychotherapy that is only just beginning to take shape. While the therapy itself has existed for a long time, it is only now that mental health authorities, regulatory bodies, and policy makers are becoming open to the idea of using these compounds for the treatment of various disorders.

The sixth chapter focused on a concept as elusive as it is important: transcendence. More specifically, it discussed the importance of a mystical experience and what it entails for the people who experience it. At the same time, it also broached a discussion around the impact of these experiences in psychotherapy. Many interesting studies are explored that have brought this discussion into the spotlight. Both these chapters are intended to give you hope, dear reader, that there are many ways in which you can seek help for the problems that you've been facing for a long time. There is light at the end of the tunnel.

In the seventh chapter, we went into the details of two journeys undertaken on psilocybin and what it means to have a safe and successful journey. The importance of using psilocybin in psychotherapy is discussed, especially with respect to its treatment of PTSD. Here, we went into the lived experiences of two women and learned from them how these journeys changed their lives forever. We also discovered lessons from their experiences that can likely enhance our own potential journeys.

The last chapter of this book dealt with the law and how it has been changing over the years. While psilocybin remains a Schedule I drug, there are many states that are decriminalizing it. At the same time, history has been made after Oregon became the first state in the US to legalize psilocybin and give it a nod for therapeutic use. Understandably, this move has caused immense excitement in researchers as well as a fair amount of trepidation. While most scientists are looking forward to a freer use of psilocybin for therapeutic purposes, there are some that are worried about history repeating itself.

All That Glitters Is Gold

We have now officially entered a new phase of psychedelic research. For the first time in decades, there is optimism among scientists, and policy makers, as well as the public, regarding these amazing compounds, and psilocybin seems to be leading this new movement. A good measure of understanding whether the future seems bright for any product or service is by seeing how the market responds to it.

In the case of psychedelics, the market is responding encouragingly. People are comparing the profitability of psychedelic stocks with those of cannabis. The fact is that, while cannabis took over a decade to truly develop in the stock market, psychedelic stocks are getting hotter within the span of a few months. Some of the stocks to look out for in the future are Delic Holdings, Field Trip, Compass Pathways, Atai Life Sciences, and Mind Medicine, among others.

If you look at the investors who are backing these stocks, you will find the biggest names in the business. For example, PayPal founder and billionaire investor Peter Thiel has invested in Compass Pathways.

It is evidently clear that the buzz around psychedelics is strong and growing in support.

The future is full of hope not only for the scientists involved in the research on psychedelics, but for each one of us. For the first time ever, we might be able to enjoy the benefits of these compounds for therapy, in a safe, open, therapeutic, and completely legal environment.

I hope that this book has helped you, dear reader, in finding hope where there was none. In the end, I ask that if this book has resonated with you, please leave a review on Amazon so that others might find it and benefit from it.

References

Carhart-Harris, Robin L. et al. "Psilocybin with Psychological Support for Treatment-Resistant Depression: An Open Label Feasibility Study." *The Lancet. Psychiatry* vol. 3,7, 2016: 619-27

Carhart-Harris, Robin L. et al. "Psilocybin for Treatment-Resistant Depression: Fmri-Measured Brain Mechanisms." *Scientific Report,* vol. 7, art. no. 13187, 13 October 2017.

Carhart-Harris, Robin L., Robert Leech, Peter J. Hellyer, Murray Shanahan, Amanda Feilding, Enzo Tagliazucchi, Dante R. Chialvo, and David Nutt. "The Entropic Brain: A Theory of Conscious States Informed by Neuroimaging Research with Psychedelic Drugs." *Frontiers in Human Neuroscience* 8 (Feb. 2014): 20. doi:10.3389/fnhum.2014.00020.

Daily, I. B. "Another Psychedelic Stock Debuts, As This One Sets Up in A Base." *Investor's Business Daily*, 2021, July 29. https://www.investors.com/news/field-trip-health-stock-debuts-adds-to-psychedelic-names-on-nasdaq/

Dass, Ram. *Be Here Now.* Lama Foundation, San Cristobal, New Mexico, 1971

Davis, A. K., Barrett, F. S., May, D. G., Cosimano, M. P., Sepeda, N. D., Johnson, M. W., Finan, P. H., & Griffiths, R. R. "Effects of Psilocybin-Assisted Therapy on Major Depressive Disorder." *JAMA Psychiatry*, 2020. https://doi.org/10.1001/jamapsychiatry.2020.3285

De Borgheyi, C. "Breaking the Mushroom Code." *Hidden in Plain Sight*, (2020). https://www.mushroomstone.com/

Deutsch, K. "15 Years of Crime Reporting Left Me with PTSD. Magic Mushrooms Helped Me Recover." *The Independent*, 13 June 2018 https://www.independent.co.uk/voices/crime-reporting-ptsd-mental-health-stress-magic-mushrooms-recovery-how-a8368946.html

Doblin, R. "Pahnke's Good Friday Experiment: A Long-Term Follow-Up and Methodologic Critique." *The Journal of Transpersonal Psychology*, vol. 23, 1991:1-28.

Doward, J. "Magic Mushrooms Could Help Ex-Soldiers to Overcome Trauma." *The Guardian*, 4 July 2020. https://www.theguardian.com/uk-news/2020/jul/04/magic-mushrooms-could-help-ex-soldiers-to-overcome-trauma

Dy, K. "A Brief History of Magic Mushrooms Across Ancient Civilizations." *Psychedelic Spotlight,* 11 August 2021. https://psychedelicspotlight.com/history-of-magic-mushrooms-across-ancient-civilizations/

Fadiman, James, Korb, Sophia "Might Microdosing Psychedelics Be Safe and Beneficial? An Initial Exploration." *Journal of Psychoactive Drugs*, 51:2, 2019, 118-122, DOI: 10.1080/02791072.2019.1593561

Goodman, E. (n.d.). "Psilocybin Mushrooms: The Window into My Subconscious." *The Seam.* https://www.the-seam.com/stories/psilocybin-mushrooms-the-window-into-my-subconscious

Griffiths, R.R., Richards, W.A., McCann, U. et al. "Psilocybin Can Occasion Mystical-Type Experiences Having Substantial and

Sustained Personal Meaning and Spiritual Significance." *Journal of Psychopharmacology* 187, 268–283, 2006. https://doi.org/10.1007/s00213-006-0457-5

Griffiths, R.R., et al. "Psilocybin Produces Substantial and Sustained Decreases in Depression and Anxiety in Patients with Life-Threatening Cancer: A Randomized Double-Blind Trial." *Journal of Psychopharmacology*, vol 12, pp. 1181–1197, 30 November 2016

Grob, C. S., Danforth, A. L., Chopra, G. S., Hagerty, M., McKay, C. R., Halberstadt, A. L., & Greer, G. R. "Pilot Study of Psilocybin Treatment for Anxiety in Patients with Advanced-Stage Cancer." *Archives of General Psychiatry*, *68*(1), 71, 2011 https://doi.org/10.1001/archgenpsychiatry.2010.116

Grof M.D., Ph.D., Stanislav. *When the Impossible Happens: Adventures in Non-Ordinary Realities.* Sounds True, Inc., Boulder, Colorado, 2006

Huxley, Aldous. *The Doors of Perception, and Heaven and Hell.* New York: Harpertorch, 2014.

Jarvie, E. "Mindset Pharma Invents Quickest, Cheapest Way to Synthesize Psilocybin." *Psychedelic Spotlight,* 3 August 2021. https://psychedelicspotlight.com/mindset-pharma-patent-quickest-cheapest-way-synthesize-psilocybin/

Jenkins, B. "The History of Magic Mushrooms." Www.fieldtriphealth.comm, 24 July 2020. https://www.fieldtriphealth.com/blog/the-history-of-magic-mushrooms

Killingsworth, M. A. and Gilbert, D. T. "A Wandering Mind Is an Unhappy Mind." *Science*, vol 330, 6006, 12 November 2010, p 932. DOI: 10.1126/science.1192439

Leary, Ph.D., Timothy, Ralph Metzner, Ph.D., Richard Alpert, Ph.D. *The Psychedelic Experience: A Manual Based on the Tibetan Book of the Dead.* Citadel Press, Secaucus, New Jersey, 1964

Macdonald, L. "What Psilocybin Taught Me About Living and Dying." *Drugscience.org.uk*, 29 January 2021. https://www.drugscience.org.uk/psilocybin-living-and-dying/

Maclean, K. A., Johnson, M. W., & Griffiths, R. R. "Mystical Experiences Occasioned by the Hallucinogen Psilocybin Lead to Increases in the Personality Domain of Openness." *Journal of Psychopharmacology*, *25*(11), 1453–1461, 2011. https://doi.org/10.1177/0269881111420188

McKenna, Terence. *Food of the Gods: The Search for the Original Tree of Knowledge.* New York: Bantam Books, 1992.

Moreno, F. A., Wiegand, C. B., Taitano, E. K., Delgado, P. L. "Safety, Tolerability, and Efficacy of Psilocybin in 9 Patients with Obsessive-Compulsive Disorder." *The Journal of Clinical Psychiatry,* 1 November 2006. https://pubmed.ncbi.nlm.nih.gov/17196053/

Nichols, David. (2020). "Psilocybin: From Ancient Magic to Modern Medicine." *The Journal of Antibiotic,* 73. 10.1038/s41429-020-0311-8, 2020

NYU Langone Health. "A Randomized Controlled Trial of the Effects of Psilocybin-Facilitated Experience on the Psychology and Effectiveness of Professional Leaders in Religion."

Clinicaltrials.gov, 24 March 2021. https://clinicaltrials.gov/ct2/show/NCT02421263

Pahnke, Walter, *Drugs and Mysticism: An Analysis of the Relationship Between Psychedelic Drugs and the Mystical Consciousness.* A thesis presented to the Committee on Higher Degrees in History and Philosophy of Religion, *Harvard University.* Cambridge, Massachusetts, June 1963.

Penrose, K. "The Power of Magic Mushrooms: My Personal Story of Healing Trauma." *Medium,* 26 March 2018. https://medium.com/@krystal_19279/the-power-of-magic-mushrooms-my-personal-story-of-healing-trauma-8aeb7d95ae29

Pollan, Michael *How to Change Your Mind: What the New Science of Psychedelics Teaches Us About Consciousness, Dying, Addiction, Depression and Transcendence.* New York: Penguin Books, 2018

Raichle, Marcus E., et al. "A Default Mode of Brain Function." *Proceedings of the National Academy of Sciences* 98, no. 2, 2001: 676–82. doi:10.1073/pnas.98.2.676.

Richards, William A. *Sacred Knowledge: Psychedelics and Religious Experiences.* New York: Columbia University Press, 2015.

Shorney, S. "I Took Part in the Psilocybin Trial and It Changed My Life." *The Independent,* 23 May 2021. https://www.independent.co.uk/independentpremium/long-reads/psychedelics-sixties-psilocybin-depression-mental-health-b1831260.html

Siebert, A. "These Four Former Pro Athletes are Using Psychedelics to Heal Their Brain Injuries." *Forbes,* 26 November 2020. https://www.forbes.com/sites/amandasiebert/2020/11/26/th

ese-four-former-pro-athletes-are-using-psychedelics-to-heal-their-brain-injuries/

Smigielski, Lukasz et al. "Psilocybin-Assisted Mindfulness Training Modulates Self-Consciousness and Brain Default Mode Network Connectivity with Lasting Effects." *NeuroImage,* Vol 196, 2019, Pages 207-215, ISSN 1053-8119, https://doi.org/10.1016/j.neuroimage.2019.04.009. (https://www.sciencedirect.com/science/article/pii/S1053811919302952)

Tierney, J. "Hallucinogens Have Doctors Tuning In Again." *The New York Times*, 12 April 2010. https://www.nytimes.com/2010/04/12/science/12psychedelics.html

Tullis, P. "How ecstasy and psilocybin are shaking up psychiatry." *Nature*, *589*(7843), 506–509, 2021. https://doi.org/10.1038/d41586-021-00187-9

Walker-Journey, J. "Psychedelics Decriminalization Bill Clears Another Hurdle in California." *Psychedelic Spotlight*, 14 July 2021. https://psychedelicspotlight.com/psychedelics-decriminalization-bill-california-clears-hurdle-controversy/

Wasson, R. Gordon. "Drugs: The Sacred Mushroom." *New York Times*, Sept. 26, 1970.

Wasson, R. Gordon. "Seeking the Magic Mushroom." *Life*, May 13, 1957, 100–120.

Wasson, R. Gordon, Albert Hofmann, and Carl A. P. Ruck. *The Road to Eleusis: Unveiling the Secret of the Mysteries*. Berkeley, Calif.: North Atlantic Books, 2008.

Wasson, Valentina Pavlovna, and R. Gordon Wasson. *Mushrooms, Russia, and History*" Vol. 2. New York: Pantheon Books, 1957.

Wikipedia. "Psilocybin decriminalization in the United States." *Wikipedia,* 8 October 2021. www.en.wikipedia.org/wiki/Psilocybin_decriminalization_in_the_United_States

Wilson, Peter Lamborn. *Ploughing the Clouds: The Search for Irish Soma.* City Lights Publishers, San Francisco, CA, 2001

Made in the USA
Middletown, DE
17 May 2023

30765405R00078